Dearest Robert,

As soon as I saw this book I
was convinced it would be a
help to me. Even after I read it
I believed strongly that you
and Darleen should have a
copy.

WITHDRAWN

Please pray for God's guidance,
understanding and wisdom as
you read this book.

May God bless you and teach
you and minister to you through
this book.

Always remember, I love you.
Renée

BEYOND SURVIVAL:

THE NEW TESTAMENT SOLUTION FOR ADULT CHILDREN OF ALCOHOLICS

143603

Jacket design and illustrations by Joe Paprocki.

Accord Books
Strang Communications Company
600 Rinehart Road
Lake Mary, FL 32746
(407) 333-0600

First Printing, March 1990
Second Printing, July 1990

Dear Children,

The chinning bar is in the door,
 The boxes on the garage floor.
Memories linger everywhere
 Of happy times we used to share.

Dear children, you will never know
 Of the love I couldn't show.
It wasn't 'cause love wasn't there.
 I just did not know how to share.

The years went by too fast for me.
 I'm just beginning now to see
That in my quest to be the best
 I burned out young—you know the rest.

You'll see in here some reasons why
 I did things that would make you cry.
I failed you so over the years
 But God reached down to dry your tears

My heart rejoices now as I
 See how His love helped you get by.
You've grown to be a blessing too.
 Others will thank God for you.

So, in this book I share with love,
 What happens when our Lord above,
Takes a messed-up life like mine
 And makes ashes begin to shine.

Because of what I learned, I do
 Want others to have more hope, too.
So pray with me that this book may
 Bring families close—the Bible way.

Love,

Mom

Table of Contents

PART III PRAYING AND HEALING:
THE DELIVERANCE PHASE

Acknowledgments

I want to thank my husband, Ken, for his patience as he endured the "fallout" that my preoccupation with this book produced; my children for their love and understanding; Lorna Sherwood, my editor (and coach), who made this readable; Ed Strang for his encouragement; my Mom and Dad who had so much to struggle through; and most of all, to Jesus Christ, who is still showing me what real love is.

Biography

Fifteen years ago Nancy Curtis would have shaken her head in disbelief had anyone told her that she was going to be in a powerful deliverance ministry. At the time Nancy tried to end her life, little did she realize that God was carefully orchestrating His own plans for her. The next decade following that suicidal incident would find her traveling across North America, appearing on national Christian radio and television networks, ministering to thousands of hurting lives.

Up to the time she attempted suicide, Nancy's life had been scarred with one grief-filled episode following another. Her earliest memories are of parents caught in the throes of alcoholic bondage, leaving her emotionally crippled. Finally, she found herself divorced, with five children to raise alone.

Then God performed a gradual miracle. A loving Savior—Jesus—took this dysfunctional *Adult Child of an Alcoholic* and began a step-by step transformation into wholeness, a process which is continuing even today.

Nancy, along with her husband, Ken, now lead the successful Spiritual Warfare Ministries, located in Lakeland, Florida. Since 1982 this dynamic team has combined teaching, testimonies and prayer to bring miracles of healing to the sick and deliverance to the oppressed.

Their ministry, "forged in the painful fires of adversity and shaped on the anvil of personal experience," sprang from the humble beginnings of a Bible study in Ken and Nancy's home.

"People just kept coming," says Nancy, "until the Bible study grew to 200 families on our sign-up list."

Needy humanity poured into their lives after it was discovered that miracles were happening. The phone and doorbell began to ring at all times of the day and night until their pastor, Karl Strader, came to their rescue. He asked Ken and Nancy to come and use the church's facilities to minister.

As their anointing increased, Ken and Nancy's ministry grew proportionately. Today, they have ministered to thousands of people across the United States, in the Bahamas and Barbados.

A vital part of Ken and Nancy's ministry includes the annual Spiritual Warfare Training Conference often held at the Masterpiece Gardens Conference Center in Lake Wales, Florida. This conference is led by a team of well-known speakers who address all aspects of spiritual warfare, from praise and worship to intercessory prayer.

People come from around the world to discover how to deal with people in bondage. They then return to their homes with the knowledge of how to set the captives free from evil spirits. These newly trained ministers of redemption continue what Nancy and Ken have started; they bring God's transforming power to the lost and hurting, turning *victims* into *victors*.

Foreword

To know Nancy is to love her. When looking into her eyes, you see the transparency of her spirit. Nancy makes herself vulnerable to the reader.

Her book is not a textbook; however, it would serve well as a textbook. It is not a novel, yet the reader is drawn into a story stranger than fiction.

The book is a must for every adult who has been a victim of a dysfunctional home. It is invaluable for every counselor, pastor or friend dealing with people of alcoholic abuse.

—Joyce Strader

(Writer for *Ministries Today* magazine,
and wife of Karl Strader, pastor
of Carpenter's Home Church
in Lakeland, Florida.)

Comments from Ex-husband

I was surprised when Nancy asked me to review the manuscript of the new book she was writing. Since I am her ex-husband, I surmised that she wanted to show it to someone she knew would be critical of her efforts, if any criticism was warranted.

We don't share the same religion, but we do share the same children; so I did feel qualified to give her my honest opinion—especially in regard to historic accuracy.

I found the book to be painfully honest and sensitive. I learned more about Nancy and her family from this book, than I did in nineteen years of marriage.

It saddened me to see how alcoholism can affect people for generations after the original episode. It helped me to understand many of the problems Nancy had to overcome from childhood through maturity.

This book should be a help to families with similar problems, and I feel that these problems are more widespread than most people realize. Nancy should be commended for her willingness to spend time, money and emotion in order to help others avoid what she had to go through.

From Husband, Ken...

For many months now, as she wrote this book, Nancy has had to recall numerous hurtful experiences while growing up in a dysfunctional family. During our years of ministry, Nancy discovered that these situations were common to many people that come from addictive families.

There is real hope for you, because the real Nancy to whom I am now married ten years, is a different person than the one I first met.

As the one who lives closest to her, I can say without reservation that she has changed. The many fears, compulsions and ungodly traits that had kept her from being "herself" left her when they were brought to light through the ministry of deliverance.

Jesus Christ changed her.

See how you, too, can be a new person—one filled with joy like Nancy is now.

—Ken Curtis

Introduction

Hi! I'm Nancy _____ and I am an
Adult Child of an Alcoholic—**but I will not be
anonymous!**

I wrote this book, because I know that what God has
done for me, He can do for anyone under the bondage
of any kind of addiction. You, too, can reach your full
potential when you understand and apply the principles
that God taught me.

A survivor. That's what I was as an *Adult Child of an
Alcoholic (ACoA),* before divine intervention opened my
eyes. Eventually I saw that the familiar trails on which
I cruised would ultimately lead to my destruction and
the downfall of those that I loved. Somehow I persevered
and made it beyond my youth, even though my environment was filled with mayhem.

This book will identify the methods I once used to sus-
tain myself while existing in a dysfunctional family. I will
describe the different coping mechanisms that all *ACoA's*
unconsciously use to face issues in which they are unable
to respond maturely. It is my desire then to show the
reader how to be free from those patterns of the past.

"How do I know whether I am a victim of a dysfunctional family?" you ask.

A dysfunctional family is one which includes one or
more members who have some type of compulsive
behavior. In my family it was alcoholism—in yours the
compulsion could be drugs such as valium, cocaine or
any mood-altering drug. Perhaps your family experienced
a member with one or a combination of several compulsive abnormalities: workaholism, sportaholism,

religious fanaticism, pornography or sexual perversion. These are all addictions of some form or another.

An addict is a person who has problems with finances, work, relationships, or health, yet still continues in that addiction. The old criteria that you have seen in the past evaluation of alcoholism/addiction described **late stage alcoholism** only.

We are going to use this insight to present a different model of alcoholism based on the Bible. At Spiritual Warfare Ministries we have seen thousands of lives changed as a result of the principles of God's Word.

> "For our struggle is not against flesh and blood,
> but against the rulers, against the authorities,
> against the powers of this dark world and against
> the spiritual forces of evil in the heavenly realms"
> (Eph. 6:12).

Most of us have been exposed to the medical model which tells us that **it is a disease talking.** Tell me, have you ever heard a disease talk? In all my years of experience as an R.N., I have not heard a single disease utter one word!

Diseases don't talk—demons do.

Those who developed the medical model shouldn't be judged harshly, because they did the best they could with the information they had, and we have learned a great deal from reading their research material about alcoholism.

This book will explore the avenue (the demonic model) that not only makes sense, but also is the *only one with real hope.*

In this book I will write often of the involvement of demons in many circumstances, so you will get used to the fact that demons are behind sick, dysfunctional and perverse behavior.

How else can you explain why eight million alcoholics live out the same script?

You see, according to the scripture, your life was not ruined by your mom or dad. You weren't abused by a *disease*, but by *demons*.

That is not bad news; it is good news, because we read in Luke 10:19: "I have given you authority to trample on snakes and scorpions and to overcome all the power of the enemy; nothing will harm you."

Survivors? Yes we are. We have been coping for years, operating at a small percentage of our potential. The task of surviving the chaos of an alcoholic environment was considerable. That is why this book was written: to present you with the fact that we don't have to be mere survivors, but we can be *more than conquerors through Jesus Christ* (Romans 8:37).

This book is not based on humanistic values or Eastern Mysticism; its foundation is the Bible, which is the only lasting source of hope. Jesus said, "I am the way and the truth and the life and there is no way to My Father except through Me." We are talking about the God of the New Testament, not the New Age. He is the God of the Christians and Jews.

It is because of my God that I am able to write this book.

Jesus rescued me from sitting in a bean bag, drinking martinis. He had mercy on me and brought me out of the New Age fast lane into a ministry that treats wounds that others have suffered, while showing them the way to get better. Jesus took me from being a middle-aged hippie, and gave me the heart of a virgin again.

PART I

Wondering and Coping:
The Denial Phase

CHAPTER ONE

Royalty in Pittsburg

I can hardly believe it yet. There Ken and I were in a helicopter dangling in mid-air over downtown Pittsburgh, while the loud thwap-thwap-thwap-thwap of chopper blades competed with the deafening roar of wind through the open doors. My heart rushed with excitement as I scanned the exhilarating view beneath us—a maze of concrete, brick and steel skyscrapers reaching up, it seemed, like welcoming arms in warm reception to our arrival. Ken hung out the open door, enthusiastically taking videos. It's a good thing he's getting pictures, I thought, our kids will never believe this.

Who *would* have ever believed that I, Nancy Curtis, a recovering *Adult Child of an Alcoholic,* would be escorted in a limousine to a meeting, or that just a few weeks later we would board an awaiting helicopter and be whisked off like royalty to speak in a packed auditorium on the outskirts of the city.

As I looked over the urban scenes that the helicopter

pilot was describing, I wondered how many souls in that huge metropolis were floundering on the brink of suicide and hell, even as I had been fifteen years earlier. How often did the Lord look down with searching eyes over this city as I was now doing?

"Father," I prayed silently, "let Ken and me make a difference for this city and for these people. Anoint the conference as only You can do, Holy Spirit."

I knew there were so many people suffering and tormented like the young woman brought to us weeks earlier by some ministers who were unable to help her.

Her appearance was shocking. Black and blue surrounded her swollen eyes, and she had numerous scratch marks on her arms and face. She had given her life to Jesus Christ two years earlier, but was obviously still very troubled.

I sat down with her and listened while her story unfolded:

"I grew up in a family where my dad molested me for many years. While in my teens I was also a victim of six different rapes. By the time I was eighteen I was an alcoholic and addicted to drugs.

"I joined the army, and in a state of rebellion while in Korea, I joined a satanic group. I became pregnant, and while I was in my seventh month of pregnancy I let them take my baby and sacrifice it in one of their rituals.

"Ever since that time I have been tormented with visions of a serpent coming toward me. When that happens, I black out. Later when I wake up, I find myself covered with these bruises and scratches."

She was convinced that someone was breaking into her apartment and beating her up while she was unconscious.

Since the ministers who attempted to help her were experienced in deliverance, I felt that the reason for her continuing torment had to be unforgiveness; so I asked her, "Tell me, how do you feel about your father?"

She responded vehemently, "I *hate* him!"

"How do you feel about the boys that raped you?"

"I HATE THEM!"

"And, how do you feel about the satanists that sacrificed your baby?"

She screamed, **"I HATE THEM TOO!"**

The root of her problem became obvious. I explained to her that she had been turned over to the tormentors because she had unforgiveness in her heart—a principle Jesus described in the parable of Matthew 18:23-35.

It wasn't strangers beating her up. It was the tormenting demons inside her using her own hands and fists to injure her body while she was in a trance.

As she began to grasp the truth, I also taught her the principle of Ephesians 6:12, helping her realize that her enemies were not her dad, her rapists or the satanists. Her enemies were demons that blinded them and used them to hurt her. Then I shared with her what Jesus said when he hung dying on the cross: "Father, forgive them. They don't know what they are doing."

The Holy Spirit began to enlighten her through the scriptures, and she understood. Leaning forward she prayed a beautiful prayer in which she told God that she forgave her daddy, the rapists and the satanists. She also forgave many others that the Holy Spirit bought to her memory.

Then, as I ministered to her, the occult demons, the violent demons, the addictive demons and the ones that were making her look so unhappy all left quickly and easily in the name of Jesus. The transformation in her countenance was astonishing. The counselors who had tried so hard to work with her watched this magnificent miracle, and we all rejoiced with her. I watched her in the services for the next several days as she glowed with her newfound peace and joy.

I knew there were thousands of others just like her in this city—human beings used by spirits to cause hurt and torment in their lives and the lives of many others. Many of them could be released if only they understood how to take the first step to freedom—forgiveness toward those who hurt them.

The helicopter's descent broke into my thoughts and turned my attention to the week just ahead—a week, as it turned out, where marvelous miracles of the Holy Spirit took place. By the end of those few short days, people were shouting from the packed auditorium, "We love you, Ken and Nancy." We turned that praise upward toward our Heavenly Father. He is really the One they saw and were expressing their love toward.

I am always amazed when Ken and I are received with such enthusiasm. The joy and excitement is almost too much to absorb, because had God not intervened when I was thirty-nine years old, I would still be feeling sorry for myself, still blaming my mom for my miserable life and still wishing that she loved me.

One dear old friend recently said, "Nancy, you've been telling me of the miracles you have seen in your ministry, but the greatest miracle I have ever seen or heard of is what happened to you!"

As I recall my childhood, I have to agree.

CHAPTER TWO

Home Sweet Home

Mom and Dad loved me, I'm sure. They did the best they could do to show it. I love them, too (Dad has been deceased more than fifteen years now), but I am angry at the devil and the way he was able to use these good, loving people to cause so much destruction.

When I was a little girl I used to watch Mom paint portraits. In those days before color film was used, photographs were painted with transparent oil colors to look like color pictures. She worked at home for years using her talent as an artist to supply extra income so my brother and I could go to parochial schools.

One of the greatest legacies Mom passed down to me was her ability to paint portraits. It must have taken her great patience to teach a young girl like me the intricacies of the art. By age sixteen I was helping her by painting the simple pictures. Most of the time the studio owners didn't know who did them. Years later this training enabled me to stay home with my babies and earn a good income while my husband was still in college.

Often her work was done begrudgingly, however.

"I have to do this because your father's printing business failed, and we need the money," I was told repeatedly.

Appreciation

On summer mornings Mom would get me up before dawn to take me golfing with her. It takes love and endurance to teach a kid to golf.

Dad taught me how to play, too. In a way, he was like a kid as he showed us how to fly kites, water-ski, catch and clean fish and enjoy camping.

During most of my childhood we had a boat that we used to take water skiing and fishing as well as on camping trips.

When Dad was going to make us a kite he would go to the hardware store, buy wood and special paper and string and make the biggest kite in the neighborhood. I remember one "masterpiece" that was too large for a child to fly. It would have taken anyone under 100 pounds right along with it, so Dad flew it while we cheered him on.

My younger brother and I also experienced the adventure of exploring the United States and a little of Mexico and Canada on our summer vacations. I can remember our excitement as we planned these summer adventures during the bleak, gray, drizzly Midwestern spring.

I especially remember the winter Mom and Dad even took us to the park with our super new toboggan and let us play until we were exhausted.

Dad made extraordinary things: snowmen, HO-scale train settings, model airplanes that could fly, and later, when I had children of my own, treehouses with trap doors and rope ladders, and slot car track models that almost filled our garage.

Christmas was always an exciting time around our house. It was a time of pretending—believing for a few brief hours that there really was a Santa Claus and that dreams do come true. But it was also a time of confusion for my childish reasoning.

When Santa Claus still brought the presents at Christmas time, I listened to the radio each night as Christmas approached—hearing of the great trip from the North Pole and arrival of Santa at the local department store. I wasn't much taller than the kitchen counter as "Gimbie and Ellie" told of Santa's progress.

"Mom, why is Santa at the other stores, too?"

I discovered boxes stuffed in closets—should I peek? And there were noises on Christmas Eve...sounds like wrapping paper...whispering...bumping and even some laughter.

I didn't understand why my friends left Santa Claus cookies and milk, and we put out beer and peanuts for him.

Pretending.

After hearing "We can't afford that," all year long, I was confused by elaborate piles of gifts around the tree.

Why were we getting things we couldn't afford?

Wow! Everything I asked for is under the tree. The beer and peanuts are gone. I think I know who Santa really is this year, but I can't let them know of my discovery.

Pretending.

I don't remember which year we stopped baking cookies together, Mom and I. But I continued making elaborate pecan fingers rolled in powdered sugar. They made the house smell good. I would bake for weeks and carefully wrap all the different colored cookies and store them in the attic. (I must have been young yet, because we still had the attic—later it was to become my bedroom.)

Christmas was pretending. Pretending for a few days that dreams do come true. Wishes can happen. Maybe we really could afford it. Maybe something magic happened.

Then reality.

How could I have understood at such a young age that those marvelous gifts were compensation to soothe parental guilt—substitutes for the love they were unable to give?

All I knew is that I looked forward to seeing all of our aunts and uncles, playing with my cousins' toys, eating the good food and enjoying the opportunity to laugh and be with happy people.

But then the pretending and enchantment of lights and tinsel faded—reality always arrived with the next sunrise.

Guilt

I have observed that those of us who grew up in *normal-looking* middle-class families doing *normal-looking* middle-class activities seem to grow up experiencing more guilt about our mixed feelings toward our parents than those who grew up in families of criminals or in ghetto neighborhoods.

Why? I struggled for years with "you sure are ungrateful," or, "there are children starving in Europe (or China)." So how could I express my feelings about my circumstances? I didn't understand emotional starvation.

Insecurity

Because of rejection and insecurity, I developed many problems, one of which was wetting the bed—not just occasionally, but almost every night.

Some of my earliest memories include dreadful nights when I would hear my parents return from the corner tavern fighting. Typically the argument degenerated until a knock-down, drag-out fight erupted.

Since I didn't want them to know that I heard them battle, I couldn't go downstairs to the bathroom—secrecy is typical in alcoholic homes—the unwritten admonition is "don't talk, don't think and don't feel."

I would go back to sleep holding my legs together hoping *"it"* wouldn't happen again.

My parents tried to get me to stop wetting the bed by shaming and threatening me. I wondered when I would *really* be sent to school with a sign on me saying I was a bed-wetter, or when they would carry out their threats to hang the sheets on the line for the neighbors to see. Never did anyone acknowledge that any fights took place, let alone associate them with my bed-wetting. The next morning it was as if nothing had happened. So I lived in dread of exposure instead of the security of unconditional love.

Until I married at age twenty, *"the problem"* still plagued me, though not every night, but very unpredictably. After a few weeks of marriage, *the most horrible thing I could think of happened. I wet the bed!* The reaction of my new husband changed my life. How? He *did not* react!

Because my husband wasn't upset with me for having this "accident," **I never wet the bed again!**

(It wasn't until I was talking with my gynecologist during my first pregnancy that I learned that insecurity was the cause of my bed-wetting. I thought he was a genius!)

Children don't know what causes their misery. In fact, children don't realize their dysfunctional home is abnormal. Even physically abused kids don't realize, while young, that normal parents don't beat their kids; they think that there is no other way to live.

The principle I discovered at the time my husband did not react to my bed-wetting is a principle that will be foundational in the healing process of an addict. That is, when you don't react to what a demon is trying to do to you when operating through another, then the demon causing that person to behave in a particular manner will have no reason to continue operating. The demon's purpose in "acting out" through someone is to cause ungodly or dysfunctional reactions in another person.

When my husband did not react in dismay to the wet bed, the demon of insecurity was undermined and had no reason to operate in me any more because it could not "push any buttons in my husband"; therefore, it ceased to operate. This is one of many ways to defeat the devil: *starve it out by not reacting to it.*

If you are reacting to the demons controlling a loved one in your life, whether they be spirits of accusation, hate, confusion, denial, addiction, domination, etc., those demons are achieving their purpose and will continue to operate. But, if you don't react, your loved one's demons don't have any more reason to continue.

This spiritual principle of "non-reaction," called *detachment* by some, has been proven to be effective when used to promote the recovery process of any abnormal behavior, whether it be bed-wetting or addiction.

Excerpts from Psalm 37

Be still before the Lord and wait patiently for him; do not fret when men succeed in their ways, when they carry out their wicked schemes. Refrain from anger and turn from wrath; do not fret—it leads only to evil. For evil men will be cut off, but those who hope in the Lord will inherit the land. A little while, and the wicked will be no more; though you look for them, they will not be found. But the meek will inherit the land and enjoy great peace. The wicked plot against the righteous and gnash their teeth at them; but the Lord laughs at the wicked, for he knows their day is coming. The wicked draw the sword and bend the bow to being down the poor and needy, to slay those whose ways are upright. But their swords will pierce their own hearts, and their bows will be broken. Better the little that the righteous have than the wealth of many wicked; for the power of the wicked will be broken, but the Lord upholds the righteous. (Psalm 37: 7-17).

The wicked lie in wait for the righteous, seeking their very lives; but the Lord will not leave them in their power or let them be condemned when brought to trial. Wait for the Lord and keep his way. He will exalt you to inherit the land; when the wicked are cut off, you will see it. I have seen a wicked and ruthless man flourishing like a green tree in its native soil, but he soon passed away and was no more; though I looked for him, he could not be found. Consider the blameless, observe the upright; there is a future for the man of peace. But all sinners will be destroyed; the future of the wicked will be cut off. The salvation of the righteous comes from the Lord; he is their stronghold in time of trouble. The Lord helps them and delivers them; he delivers them from the wicked and saves them, because they take refuge in him. (Psalm 32-40.)

PICTURE I DREW AS A YOUNG CHILD

(See Explanation on Following Page)

Expressing the Inexpressible

I guess this was about the time in my life when I decided, "Someone has to be in control around here—so it will be me."

I really never had noticed that I was not inside the house in this picture until now. It looks like I didn't want to be there, since I am outside, harassing through the window.

Why did I draw this? First of all, I never did anything disrespectful like the picture shows. Maybe I wanted to. The rest of it is accurate—Mom's sarcastic "Home Sweet Home" mentality; or should I say, her frustration, my brother's destructive behavior, the messiness, the undisciplined cat, mom's busyness and drinking—her inability to see the chaos around her. I can still remember the trails of ants walking in straight lines through the kitchen right to their food source—our cabinets.

You can see my eleven-year-old way of expressing, "Mom, can't you see? Things aren't normal around here!" Poor Mom had to work, painting portraits, because Dad had failed at his printing business and never made enough money. Anyway, that's what she told me over and over again.

Trying to describe this picture is like analyzing a dream. But I know in my heart that I was a frightened little girl. "Mom, please notice me, I need you."

It seemed that no matter how bad my brother was, excuses were made for him. At the same time, I never did anything right, or good enough.

So I probably gave up. Physically I remained at home and stayed obedient, but my heart was out the window expressing some of the feelings I couldn't express.

CHAPTER THREE

Developing Patterns of Behavior

Recreation, something most children eagerly anticipate, I learned to dread. What did I expect when we
were supposed to be having a day of fun? I learned it
always meant that I had better stay alert and watch out,
because something awful was going to happen if we went
on a picnic, camping or boating.

It is hard to demolish hope in a youngster. He will
bounce back again and again with joyous expectation for
the next great adventure. Then, little by little, like a tennis
ball, the rebound lessens, until there is no resilience left.
Many disasters had taken place before I finally refused
to get into a boat with my dad.

Childhood memories of boating, fishing and water-
skiing bring mixed emotions. We were supposed to be
enjoying ourselves, but that's not the way I recall these
events.

I don't remember having fun. Instead, I remember
anxiety and dread, because after the picnic there had to

be a terrifying ride home. After drinking all day, Dad's driving was awful, and he and Mom would usually get into a fight.

Praise God, there was a lot less traffic in the 1940's and 1950's, or I wouldn't be here to write this. It so affected me that my husband used to tease me about my inability to relax when someone else was driving the car.

Having "Fun"

One "great" day at the beach we took the boat out to an outlying island for a special remote picnic. As we were walking along the shore looking at the mating horseshoe crabs and other shore life, my brother-in-law noticed that our boat was drifting out to sea. Dad had forgotten to drop the anchor. My brother and brother-in-law tried to swim and catch it, but the current was too strong for them to intercept the boat. Dad had chosen a deserted island for this great event, so we didn't have much hope for a quick rescue.

(It's almost humorous now, but to document this continuing pattern in our family, our albums have quite a few pictures taken many different places, each having the same subject: *us in a boat being towed by someone else's boat!*)

Someone passing by that island saw our dilemma and had mercy on us. They chased down the boat and brought it back. We were again safe until the next time.

And the next time, as I remember it, my husband and I had to get out of the boat and grab a rope and pull the boat across a sand bar to maneuver it into water deep enough to return to the dock. Dad had forgotten that the tide had gone out since we had used that pass. We could even observe the waterfowl standing in the water, not

34

swimming on it. Yet, a drinking dad couldn't comprehend that *standing birds meant shallow water.*

Another beautiful day of relaxation was ruined one time because Dad towed his sailboat, with the mast still up, through a county park toward the boat-ramp. I don't know how he got there from his house, but the mast tore down the power lines in the park, making dozens of families very unhappy with him.

Of course, every disaster precipitated a fight. I got so I was programmed to expect a fight to follow anything that was supposed to be fun. (Maybe that was why Mom walked in on me one day when I was still a fourth grader and said, "I never heard of a fourth grader being nervous." I was just being hypervigilant, checking my environment continuously to see what I could do to prevent the next disaster.)

How many of you readers are still that way?

Anxiety

Camping was another family activity. I have always loved nature: little animals, fish, water, wind and sunshine. So camping created a great deal of conflict within me—a love for the outdoors on the one hand, and a detestation for the fighting I associated with it on the other.

One weekend we decided on a Northern Wisconsin site. It was a beautiful woodsy place, and I helped set up the campsite, eagerly anticipating the enjoyable week that lay ahead. My peace was ruined when Mom sat down on the folding chair and folded her finger between the crossed legs. Dad took her to the hospital, and all I heard the rest of the trip was how her finger wouldn't stop bleeding and that her blood didn't clot right. I spent the rest of the "vacation" observing her anxiously because I thought she was going to bleed to death.

Manipulation

Death. I was often reminded by Mom that she was going to die soon. Perhaps that was how she was able to manipulate me into being so helpful—I didn't want her to die of a heart attack. Several nights I lay awake most of the night praying for her to live because she was having angina pectoris. To a little kid that sounds awesome. (Actually she has been in super health and at age seventy was still able to play eighteen holes of golf with me.)

Another time she was supposedly dying of pneumonia. Dad took me to watch a professional tennis match while she lay home in bed with that pneumonia. I didn't enjoy a minute of the match.

If my brother and I would get into a fight while doing the dishes, Mom would make a statement like, "When I am in my grave you will be sorry." Whenever we misbehaved we were controlled with statements contrived to make us feel like we were "killing her" and would really regret it, because she wasn't going to be with us for very long.

In some cultures a statement is often made, "You'll be the death of me yet." What does that statement do to the child? Have you noticed that some of those children grow up to be super achievers? Have you also observed that they seem to be **driven** by some force?

Rejection

When I was still quite small, I remember my First Communion as a very special time. I was very aware of Jesus and aware that the prayer I said to renounce Satan was powerful. I felt very holy and spent the afternoon standing at the bus stop on the street corner with my hands folded, wearing my white dress and veil. I wanted everyone to see how holy I was.

36

Back home my family was having a big drinking party which I had messed up. I had walked into the living room and saw all the hors d'oeuvres on a Lazy Susan. I thought it would make a nice wheel, so I grabbed the edge and gave it a spin that sent all the little sandwiches flying *all* over the room.

I knew my mom was furious with me for messing up her snacks. As young as I was, I could tell that I was in the way, so I wandered up to the bus stop and acted holy.

Withdrawal

I learned at a very young age how to get Mom to pay attention to me: I would get sick. I recall *purposely exposing myself to the mumps when they were going around*. Finally I succeeded!

You see, when I got sick Mom would take off from work and bring me milk shakes from the corner drug store. So in addition to mumps, I caught whooping cough, pneumonia and what they called "symptoms of polio." As a fourth grader I spent a whole month in bed with a stiff neck. I also had so many sore throats that I developed a penicillin allergy by the time I reached high-school age.

Yet, when I reached puberty, I didn't let Mom know. Somehow I had two menstrual periods without understanding what was happening. I finally asked her what to do about the problem when the third one came around. I was only ten.

About that same time my drinking started, too. Each month I would get cramps, which my family called "mullygrups." I would get so sick that I would vomit. I usually had to spend at least a day in bed, or on the ground if we were at some family outing.

Mom discovered that I felt better if she gave me some

brandy. I *did*—so she did. When I was a very little girl the pattern began to develop when I became sick and Mom would take time out to get me milkshakes. As I grew older it switched to Mom getting me a drink when I felt ill.

She wouldn't buy a bra for me until I had developed into a size 36C. Can you image the teasing a sixth grader would have to endure, being the only one in the class with huge, bouncing breasts?

Of course, Mom was not responsible for my early puberty. What I'm trying to illustrate is that an *alcoholic doesn't notice the obvious.* An alcoholic is so focused on getting his next drink that his child can be mature for months before being noticed.

Mom loved me, but the demons using her were trying to destroy me: "The thief *[devil]* comes only to steal and kill and destroy; I *[Jesus]* have come that they may have life, and have it to the full" (John 10:10).

My Room

It wasn't until recently that I realized my childhood bedroom was unusual. Dad always meant well, but he couldn't finish things. He started to remodel the attic, the unfinished product becoming my very own bedroom. In fact, Mom and Dad surprised me by giving me my own twin bed and brand new mattress set.

At last, the stained, urine-soaked purple studio couch with its dank, pungent odor was pitched out, and for the first time in my life I slept in my own bed. This, I was told, was to stay dry; so void of a mattress cover, the rubber sheet became a convenient weapon to shame me out of wetting the bed. Needless to say, try as I might, the bed did not stay dry.

So what was unusual about my bedroom? No heat, for

example. Winters could get very cold in the Midwest. Sometimes the temperature got down to thirty-five degrees below zero, and I would freeze upstairs in the attic. There was no air intake and no circulation; therefore, the room stayed cold.

I left a glass of water out one night to see what would happen. It froze solid. No wonder I would crawl in bed at night and shiver under the covers for hours before I could get to sleep. *I didn't know this was abnormal, even though all my friends had warm bedrooms.* I already was so demolished emotionally that I didn't think I was supposed to have warmth.

Finally I discovered that if I dragged my bed to a hole in the floor where some heat would drift upward, I could hang my foot over the side to let some warm air under the blanket. After trying to sleep in that position all night, it was still cold. No wonder the nuns at school were always on my case for underachievement. I tested out with a high IQ but I wasn't "working up to my ability"—I was tired!

Earning Love

One Sunday morning, when I was about seven, Mom and Dad were too "hungover" to get up for church. I got my brother dressed and we walked the one-and-a-half miles to church. When we returned Mom had a fit because I had embarrassed her by going to church in a skirt and blouse that didn't match. (And I was so very proud of myself for being able to pick out the orange plaid blouse and the skirt with pretty pink plaid.) I couldn't win.

I reasoned that if I tried harder she would love me. So I cleaned out the green and black mold growing in the refrigerator. I went down to the basement and did all the laundry. Apparently I must have done that right, because it then became my permanent job from age ten, along with the responsibility of cooking for our family.

One day I decided to make a beautiful beef roast dinner with all the trimmings. I started after school and timed it to be done when my parents were expected home from work. At 7:00 p.m. they still weren't home. The oven regulator didn't work well enough to keep the roast on warm, so when they finally did come home drunk, they yelled and screamed at me for ruining a roast that cost them so much money—and all I had wanted to do was to surprise them and make them happy.

The desire to cook probably came from hunger. I can remember waiting one Sunday afternoon for my parents to come home from the corner tavern so they could get dinner for my brother and me. When they didn't come home, I took my brother and together we peeked through the windows of all six taverns near us, hoping to find them.

We couldn't locate them, though, because it was light outside and the taverns were dark inside. We gave up and came home. When they returned they again had a fit because we embarrassed them by looking for them in the taverns. So I learned to cook.

Escape

In my seventh grade God intervened, I know, by getting me involved in music. I was so depressed that one of the nuns took pity on me and gave me an old trombone, telling me that the school orchestra needed a trombone player. I took that old horn, and despite Mom's complaints rising up the stairway because of wrong notes, this time I wouldn't be squelched.

That trombone was a major vehicle of my stabilization,

for a while, in high school. I know it was God's gift, because He had given me a love of and talent for music. Prior to that, singing in the choir had been one of the most fulfilling activities in which I had participated. Music, especially church music, made me feel good, much in the same way King Saul of the Old Testament was soothed by David's harp (see 1 Samuel 16:23).

Before I was aware of how God was guiding me, He gave me a means to escape and the opportunity to feel I was a part of something. He caused me to feel valuable, talented and even worthwhile. After all, girls didn't usually play trombones, so I felt very special.

I played in the grade-school and high-school orchestra and marched in the high-school drum and bugle corps— in parades, contests, games and, best of all, the city's Catholic Symphony Orchestra.

In the first symphony concert I played, I had to wear my aunt's dress because all the women wore formals. I felt so out of place, a thirteen-year-old wearing a see-through black lace dress with a flesh-colored slip underneath. So again I had to endure ridicule because no one had provided me with a modest, youthful-looking dress.

Later in life, after a ten-year break and the birth of five children, when I really needed a diversion I picked up my trombone once again. With the encouragement of the orchestra director in our city, I again played in a symphony and continued for five more years. Music has given me great memories. It was not a spiritual solution, but it helped me get through some difficult phases of life.

God gave you opportunities to escape your sick environment, too, or you wouldn't have been able to survive it. To this day music really ministers to me. I am very sensitive to good music and, conversely, also very sensitive to bad music. It was the bad music that opened the door for Satan later to bring confusion and chaos into my marriage.

When I describe my childhood, I'm describing a family who owned a car, a boat, a tent and house in a very pleasant middle-class neighborhood. I know that those of you that had to live in ghetto neighborhoods had it much worse that I did. But I was wounded from rejection just like you. I needed to count on some kind of consistency in life—like you—but I thought there was no one to depend upon but me. That's what I was being forced to believe.

So I made some decisions:

1. *When I grow up I will never be like my mother.* I wasn't. I was **worse!** "Do not judge, or you too will be judged. For in the same way you judge others, you will be judged, and with the measure you use, it will be measured to you" (Matthew 7:1,2). I judged her and I ended up being likewise judged.

2. At age twelve I determined *I'm going to accomplish so much that they will be proud of me. Then they will love me.*

3. *Someone around here has to be in charge, so I will take control.* That is when I took a new role upon myself—a "coping mechanism" which is typical for an ACoA. I decided *I must **always** be in **control.***

CHAPTER FOUR

Floundering

Children who are raised in a dysfunctional family adapt to certain "roles" in order to fill a need for peace and security in that family. They adopt these roles in an attempt to ensure emotional survival.

When we become adults, these "coping mechanisms" actually are the roots of certain drives which become the main motivating factors in our successes or failures in life.

My brother, for example, took on the role of *The Rebel* (called Scapegoat by many authorities). I was afraid of getting into trouble, but my brother was a daredevil. His inner motivation was probably one protecting the family secrets. The rationalization of *The Rebel's* behavior goes something like this: "If I can divert attention to myself, nobody will ever find out about the dysfunctional behavior in my family."

A secondary benefit to this behavior was, *he did get attention!* Then, whenever he got into trouble, with parking tickets, school officials or the police, my mother

would bail him out. This classic family response—
The Enabler response—is a characteristic role in and
of itself, or combines with other behavioral patterns.
(I wish Mom would have known about Dr. James
Dobson's book, *Love Must Be Tough,* so that my mother
and brother could have learned that negative consequences should follow negative behavior.)

Along with *The Enabler* role, my mother played *The
Poor Victim* in our family. Later I would find myself
repeating her patterns of "martyrdom."

Dad watched all of this occurring, but in order to avoid
any conflict with my mother, he remained *The Passive-
Invisible* one. To be noticed meant having to make
decisions. To make decisions meant having to take
responsibility. Dad had probably been passive from childhood, a typical *Ahab*, while Mom was more like *Jezebel*
in their relationship, and his absence wounded me as
much as Mom's presence.

I picked up *The Passive-Invisible* role in grade
school. I didn't want to be noticed, and I wouldn't raise
my hand to answer questions even when I was sure I
knew the answer. I dreaded winning a spelling bee, because that meant I would be the only remaining one;
therefore, I would be noticed. So I preferred losing to
being obvious.

At that age I did not realize that the classmate who was
The Comedian was playing out his own role. It was
usually a boy, and he would say anything to get a laugh.
The Comedian goes through life desperate for attention, trying to bury his pain in a shallow grave of jokes.
Later in life, this type of person is unable to participate
in a serious discussion, substituting jokes for meaningful
dialogue.

Many families have what I call *The Rescuer*. He
explains what Mom *really* meant to Brother, or clarifies

what Brother said to Dad. Often he will become a counselor, minister or psychologist; but unknowingly he is driven by the need to "fix everyone." These people also become great nurses, good in crisis-oriented professions simply because they have had so much experience with a multitude of crises growing up.

I became a nurse, but it wasn't entirely because I was *The Rescuer* type. Instead I adapted to what I now call *The Controller* role. I had a real need to be a hero.

Someone has to take charge around here, I had decided. Yes, I would be the one in our family who got things done. By age ten I did the laundry and could cook and shop for groceries. Since it was embarrassing to bring friends into our house, I had learned to clean it myself.

As a child I would try my best to scrub the kitchen floor until it glimmered. Mom would always spot a corner I missed, and a tirade would follow. I've unconsciously blocked out the verbiage, but the resulting decision I remember clearly: *I've got to be perfect to be loved.* Therefore, I would either be compulsive or I would procrastinate, because I dreaded criticism. I could put off facing it if I delayed a chore long enough. In fact, I never wrote a thank you note to anyone because I didn't want the person to read it and dislike the way I wrote it. So, being unable to tolerate the possibility of more rejection, I didn't write any notes at all.

If *The Controller* procrastinates long enough to avoid the reaction that he fears, he can maintain the illusion of being in charge.

After marriage, my procrastination motivated my patient mother-in-law to come over during my second pregnancy and show me how I could wipe off window-sills with a rag and a bucket, etc. I was so mortified that I was not "in charge" and had not "performed" to perfection; but I was also grateful that she cared enough to teach me some housekeeping skills.

Those of us who decided to take charge as youngsters are usually quite competent leaders in life. Most of us remain unaware that underneath this great ability is the fear that **if I ever lose control, it will all come apart.**

Demonic influence is obvious in the overt behavior of **The Rebel** but is much less obvious when dealing with **The Comedian** or **The Passive-Invisible.** This influence is hardly obvious at all in the defense mechanisms of **The Rescuer, Enabler, Victim,** or **Controller.** We fall through the cracks and don't show up in the counselor's office, because we seem to be getting along just fine in life.

Warts

At a young age I felt so much responsibility for the stability of my family that the burden physically manifested itself as warts. The stress of the fighting and the continuous inability to handle household obligations caused me to develop hundreds of flat warts all over my body and face.

So my warts made me feel like even more of an oddball. A dermatologist with gobs of stinky salve didn't cure the warts, so Mom gave up on the M.D. and made one of the gravest errors of my childhood. Unknowingly she brought a curse upon my life by using occult power to get rid of the warts.

The hypnotist was a strange sort of person who stared into my eyes as he told me that my hideous growths would be gone in twenty-one days, if I drank the peppermint drops mixed with water *exactly* according to the routine he prescribed.

I was "cured" by this occult method, but it was not

the "power of suggestion" that cured me. Hypnotism opens one up to supernatural healing, and the source of that supernatural power is Satan. My "cure" was like jumping from the frying pan into the fire. Almost immediately, I got fat.

First Timothy 4:1 gives a warning against occult activity: "The Spirit clearly says that in later times some will abandon the faith and follow deceiving spirits and things taught by demons."

"...evil men and impostors will go from bad to worse, deceiving and being deceived" (2 Timothy 3:13).

The first commandment warns us not to follow after other gods (other sources of supernatural power). If we do, we bring a curse upon ourselves, our children, our grandchildren and our great grandchildren. How awful!

Mom took me to a man who used occult power (supernatural power that was not reached through prayer in the name of Jesus.) When another god, (the source of the supernatural healing power) was sought for healing, I was cursed. Just **one** of the manifestations of that curse was getting fat.

Hosea 4:6 says that God's people are being "destroyed from lack of knowledge." How sad that my family didn't understand the Bible and unknowingly sought help several times from demonic sources.

Many families are suffering needlessly because of occult activity in their background. Out of desperation, families of addicts and the addicts themselves seek help from whatever group or person is convenient at the time. Unfortunately, most support groups are New Age, humanistic or overtly occultic. As a result, many addicts and their families remain in bondage to problems far worse than the original situation—due to the results of being cursed.

One of my friends, for example, attended Al-Anon and

became involved in astrology and metaphysics. She started out as an atheist and then found her "higher power" in the occult.

Bible Warnings

In order to help someone get free and stay free from the demonic influences of family curses, I have carefully listed the curses found in the Old Testament so that you can be informed concerning them. Although the list is lengthy, please study it so you can comprehend the full impact of what a curse will do:

"However, if you do not obey the LORD your God and do not carefully follow all his commands and decrees I am giving you today, all these curses will come upon you and overtake you:

"You will be cursed in the city and cursed in the country.

"Your basket and your kneading trough will be cursed.

"The fruit of your womb will be cursed, and the crops of your land, and the calves of your herds and the lambs of your flocks.

"You will be cursed when you come in and cursed when you go out.

"The LORD will send on you curses, confusion and rebuke in everything you put your hand to, until you are destroyed and come to sudden ruin because of the evil you have done in forsaking him. The LORD will plague you with diseases until he has destroyed you from the land you are entering to possess. The LORD will strike you with wasting disease, with fever and inflammation, with scorching heat and drought, with blight and mildew, which will plague you until you perish. The sky over your head will be bronze, the ground beneath you iron. The LORD will turn the rain of your country into dust and powder; it will come down from the skies until you are destroyed.

"The LORD will cause you to be defeated before your enemies. You will come at them from one direction but flee from them in seven, and you will become a thing of horror to all the kingdoms on earth. Your carcasses will be food for all the birds of the air and the beasts of the earth, and there will be no one to frighten them away. The LORD will afflict you with the boils of Egypt and with tumors, festering sores and the itch, from which you cannot be cured. The LORD will afflict you with madness, blindness and confusion of mind. At midday you will grope about like a blind man in the dark. You will be unsuccessful in everything you do; day after day you will be oppressed and robbed, with no one to rescue you.

"You will be pledged to be married to a woman, but another will take her and ravish her. You will build a house, but you will not live in it. You will plant a vineyard, but you will not even begin to enjoy its fruit. Your ox will be slaughtered before your eyes, but you will eat none of it. Your donkey will be forcibly taken from you and will not be returned. Your sheep will be given to your enemies, and no one will rescue them. Your sons and daughters will be given to another nation, and you will wear out your eyes watching for them day after day, powerless to lift a hand. A people that you do not know will eat what your land and labor produce, and you will have nothing but cruel oppression all your days. The sights you see will drive you mad. The LORD will afflict your knees and legs with painful boils that cannot be cured, spreading from the soles of your feet to the top of your head.

"The LORD will drive you and the king you set over

you to a nation unknown to you or your fathers. There you will worship other gods, gods of wood and stone. You will become a thing of horror and an object of scorn and ridicule to all the nations where the LORD will drive you.

"You will sow much seed in the field but you will harvest little, because locusts will devour it. You will plant vineyards and cultivate them but you will not drink the wine or gather the grapes, because worms will eat them. You will have olive trees throughout your country but you will not use the oil, because the olives will drop off. You will have sons and daughters but you will not keep them, because they will go into captivity. Swarms of locusts will take over all your trees and the crops of your land.

"The alien who lives among you will rise above you higher and higher, but you will sink lower and lower. He will lend to you, but you will not lend to him. He will be the head, but you will be the tail.

"All these curses will come upon you. They will pursue you and overtake you until you are destroyed, because you did not obey the LORD your God and observe the commands and decrees he gave you. They will be a sign and a wonder to you and your descendants forever. Because you did not serve the LORD your God joyfully and gladly in the time of prosperity, therefore in hunger and thirst, in nakedness and dire poverty, you will serve the enemies the LORD sends against you. He will put an iron yoke on your neck until he has destroyed you.

"The LORD will bring a nation against you from far away, from the ends of the earth, like an eagle swooping down, a nation whose language you will not understand, a fierce-looking nation without respect for the old or pity for the young. They will devour the young of your livestock and the crops of your land until you are destroyed. They will leave you no grain, new wine or oil, nor any calves of your herds or lambs of your flocks until you are ruined. They will lay siege to all the cities throughout your land until the high fortified walls in which you trust fall down. They will besiege all the cities throughout the land the LORD your God is giving you.

"Because of the suffering that your enemy will inflict on you during the siege, you will eat the fruit of the womb, the flesh of the sons and daughters the LORD your God has given you. Even the most gentle and sensitive man among you will have no compassion on his own brother or the wife he loves or his surviving children, and he will not give to one of them any of the flesh of his children that he is eating. It will be all he has left because of the suffering your enemy will inflict on you during the siege of all your cities. The most gentle and sensitive woman among you—so sensitive and gentle that she would not venture to touch the ground with the sole of her foot—will begrudge the husband she loves and her own son or daughter the afterbirth from her womb and the children she bears. For she intends to eat them secretly during the siege and in the distress that your enemy will inflict on you in your cities.

"If you do not carefully follow all the words of this law, which are written in this book, and do not revere this glorious and awesome name—the LORD your God—the LORD will send fearful plagues on you and your descendants, harsh and prolonged disasters, and severe and lingering illnesses. He will bring upon you all the diseases of Egypt that you dreaded, and they will cling to you. The LORD will also bring on you every kind of sickness and disaster not recorded in this Book of the Law, until you are destroyed. You who were as numerous as the stars in the sky will be left but few in number, because you did not obey the LORD your God. Just as it pleased the LORD to make you prosper and increase in number, so it will please him to ruin and destroy you. You will be uprooted from the land you are entering to possess.

"Then the LORD will scatter you among all nations, from one end of the earth to the other. There you will worship other gods—gods of wood and stone, which neither you nor your fathers have known. Among those nations you will find no repose, no resting place for the sole of your foot. There the LORD will give you an anxious mind, eyes weary with longing, and a despairing heart. You will live in constant suspense, filled with dread both night and day, never sure of your life. In the morning you will say, 'If only it were evening!' and in the evening, 'If only it were morning!'—because of the terror that will fill your hearts and the sights that your eyes will see. The LORD will send you back in ships to Egypt on a journey I said you should never make again. There you will offer yourselves for sale to your enemies as male and female slaves, but no one will buy you" (Deuteronomy 28:15-68).

Cursed?

What do you think of that? Perhaps you can understand why you or your family have suffered so. You may have been locked into a role and unable to successfully overcome destructive behavior and habits as a result of a curse.

If you or your ancestors have sought help from other gods (demons) in a quest for information, peace, healing or prosperity, then you were cursed.

Seeking after another god (whether he be called "a higher power," "divinity," "ascended master," "the man upstairs," or even "god" by a spiritist, New Ager, etc.) without coming through Jesus Christ, will put you in contact with a demon power and under the bondage of a curse.

It is dangerous to join any group that alludes to "god" but does not have a firm New Testament base. Jesus said, "I am the way and the truth and the life. No one comes to the Father except through me" (John 14:6).

CHAPTER FIVE

Worm to Butterfly

To a twelve-year-old the three-month gap between grade school and high school is a long time. There was no junior high then, so I took a good, long look at myself that summer and decided that high school represented an opportunity for a new beginning for me.

You see, grade school had been a disaster. I smelled funny, grew up too soon, was embarrassed in class by the paper boy who told everyone what our home was like and, worst of all, I was fat.

The private Catholic girls' school that I would be attending in the fall was not in my neighborhood. I gained renewed hope in that I would be surrounded by new people that didn't know my past. I could start over in life.

What I did that summer was ceremonial, but I didn't know it then. In the empty lot next door I dug a fort with a tunnel. It was near a very large lilac bush, and every day I went out with the shovel and dug. What I didn't realize was that all the digging was getting me into good physical shape. I went into that hole a caterpillar and came out transformed, a butterfly. (I must have done a lot of thinking as I sat in the hole, because I remember being alone in there for long periods of time.)

Twenty-five pounds lighter, with a new short, neat haircut I started my high school career.

Brownie Points

Superachievers like myself don't get counseling in high school. We tend to deny a lot about ourselves, putting on lots of mileage before the holes in our psyche show up years later. No one noticed the deep insecurities I carried—I was too busy gathering "successes" to cover them over. If no one else could see them, maybe I could convince myself they didn't exist.

I must say that I had a lot of fun in high school. I played trombone in two orchestras, marched in the drum and bugle corps, dated every weekend after age sixteen, was art editor of the yearbook staff, marched in parades, and went to many proms. It looked like sadness, loneliness and depression were behind me, but I continued the fruitless attempts to please my parents.

When I got my first job at age sixteen, I used the money to buy Mom a watch which I hung on the Christmas tree, because I wanted so much for her to love me. Then I bought her a clothes dryer to ease her burden. We had agreed that I would use the room and board money she normally charged me for dryer payments. We ended up fighting about the money. We fought a lot about money. I would put most of my earnings in the bank and she would always tell me to spend it and enjoy life.

While a senior in high school two different messages about my future were strongly conveyed to me by my mother:

(1) "Nancy, you should travel all around the world while you are still young" and (2) "Nancy, nice girls don't go to college away from home."

So I got a job as a laboratory technician, did not go to college or travel anywhere, and saved my money to get married instead. The mixed messages were too confusing.

In the meantime, the invisible roots of bitterness fed by years of unforgiveness, insidiously, secretly, grew deep within me. I had suppressed the anger and resentment so long that it had become a familiar part of me. Added to that was the suppressed grief that too quickly my childhood was gone—I had to be so grown up when others still basked in the carefree atmosphere that childhood normally provides.

Childhood Lost

Most of us have not yet grieved over our lost childhood. In fact, many of you may not be aware that the source of your inability to have fun is that you have never been able to express grief over that loss. That's denial again, complicated with guilt.

Most of us have gone through much of our life before realizing that we had lost something so precious, the opportunity to be carefree while young. Others of you have lost your virginity. Don't suppress the anger and resentment any more. Be mad, but focus your anger at the one to blame, the devil.

Buried resentment makes us sick, a fact proven medically and scripturally. We are the only ones who lose if we deny those feelings and bury them.

What needs to be done? We need to face the past, not run from it. I tried to run. Don't stay too busy to let it bother you. Don't drown it in alcohol. Quit denying your hurt. God understands. The important thing to remember is that your mom or dad are not the ones who ruined your life. Your enemy is a demon power that used your parents to try to destroy you. Always keep in mind, even while you are grieving over your loss, that once you are able to admit anger, grief, resentment and bitterness, there is a next step to freedom: forgiveness.

Bitterness to Sweet Release

There is a new branch of medicine called psycho-neuroimmunology that has researched the cause of sickness. They claim that almost one hundred percent of all diseases are caused by stress. And what is the major source of stress? The devil. (One Adult Child of an Alcoholic stated, "As I speak, they live in my head.") He was referring to his parents, but in reality he was hearing demons in his head (the same ones that used his parents) who were harassing him because of what he suffered while young. So we are dealing with buried hate, resentment, hurt feelings, or whatever is your favorite word for your reaction from the abuse in your life.

In Matthew 18 Jesus explains what happens to us when we haven't forgiven those who hurt us—we're turned over to the tormentors:

"Therefore, the kingdom of heaven is like a king who wanted to settle accounts with his servants. As he began the settlement, a man who owed him ten thousand talents was brought to him. Since he was not able to pay, the master ordered that he and his wife and his children and all that he had be sold to repay the debt.

"The servant fell on his knees before him. 'Be patient with me,' he begged, 'and I will pay back everything.' The servant's master took pity on him, canceled the debt and let him go.

"But when that servant went out, he found one of his fellow servants who owed him a hundred denarii. He grabbed him and began to choke him. 'Pay back what you owe me!' he demanded.

"His fellow servant fell to his knees and begged him, 'Be patient with me, and I will pay you back.'

"But he refused. Instead, he went off and had the man thrown into prison until he could pay the debt. When the other servants saw what had happened, they were greatly distressed and went and told their master everything that had happened.

"Then the master called the servant in. 'You wicked servant,' he said, 'I canceled all that debt of yours because you begged me to. Shouldn't you have had mercy on your fellow servant just as I had on you?' In anger his master turned him over to the jailers to be tortured, until he should pay back all he owed.

"This is how my heavenly Father will treat each of you unless you forgive your brother from your heart" (Matthew 18:23-35).

That is why some have psychosomatic disorders. One of the roots of compulsive behavior is pain that is buried. Pretending that it isn't there or that it doesn't bother you anymore won't solve your problems. Stoicism isn't the answer. *Facing your past and forgiving those who wounded you is the only lasting solution.*

Satan blinded my Mom and Dad and they really didn't know what they were doing. If they really did, they wouldn't have chosen booze over me. As this principle of forgiveness was explained to me, I was able to forgive them by following the example Jesus set for us from the cross, "Father, forgive them for they do not know what they are doing" (Luke 23:34).

Let me encourage you to take step number one: Face your past as God unfolds the awareness of it.

Statistics show that a large percentage of us have periods of loss of memory from our childhood. That is often a sign that we were abused and had to block the memory to survive.

When buried memories surface, they need to be dealt with. It is important to forgive the parent who hurt you *and* the one who didn't protect you from the hurt.

Let me encourage you to pray and release forgiveness today. I have included the following prayer for a guideline:

> *"Dear God, until now I've not been able to understand a lot of things about my parents. I've been so confused. Now Lord, to the best of my ability, I forgive _____ and _____. I know now that whey were blinded by Satan and didn't know what they were doing. I tear up the IOU and I forgive them now. I will no longer hold it against them.*
>
> *"Thank you, Lord, for setting me free as I have set them free. This I pray in Jesus' name. Amen."*

Expect some emotional cleansing to follow this prayer of forgiveness; physical healing often will follow also.

Every week in our ministry I am giving someone permission to cry. Jesus wept before He raised Lazarus from the dead. Weeping is a scriptural process toward healing—after the grieving, the resurrection—the new life. (See John 11:34-44.)

What kind of baggage—demonic strongholds from the past—have we brought into adult life? Fear, rejection and perfection for example? What coping mechanisms? Denial or busyness maybe? What is the source of these coping mechanisms? Demons. How do they trip us up today? Misunderstanding, paranoia, sensitivity and isolation. How did they yesterday? Failure and denial. How will they next year? They won't if they are uncovered. The Bible says that people perish from lack of knowledge.

Spiritual Warfare Ministries, the ministry God has entrusted to my husband and me, is sometimes called the "V.D. clinic of the church" because the "germs"—demons—are exposed. People's lives won't be destroyed by entities that they can't see, if they know the truth.

We can rise above mere survival. In fact, we can be more than conquerors through Jesus Christ.

CHAPTER SIX

Repeating the Patterns

My family was extremely prejudiced. I'm of German-Irish descent, and my parents degraded other cultures with ugly, slang labels. Those people who lived in segregated cultural communities different from ours were all belittled by my parents—some of them for being too rich, some of them for being too dirty, and others for being too preoccupied with cleaning their houses.

One of the worst things I could have done to hurt my parents was to date and marry a boy from a culture they condemned. My decision may have been contaminated with rebellion, too; I don't know. But I really loved him.

Anyway, I made a decision that I would not be prejudiced against blacks or any of those other people that I heard them criticize. I saw prejudice as a hateful thing. I always felt empathy for minorities because I, too, was a minority.

I was a minority in our school because I was different. I probably smelled bad from wetting the bed; I didn't discover until I was older that I could shower every morning. I was overweight and just didn't "fit."

Our grade school class had about thirty-five students. Do you remember being in a classroom that size where there was one kid who was different. Really different? Smart maybe, but different? That was me.

I refused to participate in prejudice and racism, which was the only pathological behavioral pattern that I am aware of in my parents which I did not repeat—but I shudder now to realize it was the only one, despite my efforts to be different.

Determination

"I WILL NEVER BE LIKE MY MOTHER WHEN I GROW UP!"

At the time I made that statement I was sure that I wouldn't be like her when I became a mom. **I wasn't. I was worse!**

I wouldn't become crabby or get drunk, I thought. I wasn't going to be the kind of mother who would only talk to her kids about basics in life after a couple of drinks, like the time Mom instructed me in the "facts of life."

One day, before I went to babysit, Mom decided to prepare me for the job. Changing a baby's diaper was the subject. I stood there shifting from one foot to the other as Mom slurred, "Boys wet up the front, and girls wet up the back." Poor Mom—apparently she felt more at ease with me after a few drinks. *"I'm not going to be that way,"* I thought.

I had judged and said, "I'm not going to be like her." I didn't know the Bible had a warning that I would end up just like the one I judged. (Matthew 7:1-2).

What happened? I didn't recognize the trap of *denial*

64

that was operating in my life. My greatest determination didn't prevent me from repeating Mom's mistakes.

I was determined to be a good wife and mother. While my new husband attended college, I learned to sew as a result of our frugal budget, making most of my clothes and the children's clothes as they came along.

Some of the most precious times in my life were when my children were born and I could share intimate moments with my nursing babies. I breastfed the first until he had hernia surgery at six weeks of age. After I developed a severe case of mastitis during my baby boy's hospital stay, the doctor informed me that I could never nurse a baby again.

ACoC's can have a great deal of determination when they want, so when we moved to a different state, I kept the information regarding the mastitis a secret from my new doctor. Gleefully I nursed my fourth and fifth babies.

I was a great cook and avid gardener, raising many vegetables while the children were young. I mowed the lawn, painted the car and trained the children to cook and do their own laundry. I was a chauffeur for 4-H, music lessons, swimming team, soccer, ceramics, golf, cross country, little league football and tennis. Later on I got involved in Junior Woman's Club, Sunday School teaching, choir, Pre-Cana teaching and the Garden Club.

Addiction!

I was never going to be like my mother, so during my first pregnancy, when the doctor prescribed diet pills to prevent excessive weight gain, I *denied* my susceptibility and was easily hooked on amphetamines.

In those days there were no prescription-drug controls and I became thoroughly addicted. By my third pregnancy, the doctors on the base where we were stationed had prescribed enough diet pills for me to keep stashed around the house—just like alcoholics hide liquor.

In the meantime, my husband had earned his doctorate and we had moved to captain's quarters on the SAC base. The culture shock of moving from a poor, run-down urban neighborhood compared to the prestige of being a doctor's wife kept me dependent on the speed—a crutch to give me the energy and courage to impress people. I was driven by my pathological need to be seen as a great achiever.

They all wondered how a mother of three babies could train a Weimaraner, raise Siamese kittens, refinish furniture, have great parties and still have time to raise the kids. They didn't know my "secret."

By the time we moved to Florida my health had deteriorated from substance abuse. I didn't know anyone in the new town and I had no drive to impress anyone, so I decided to quit the drugs and rest. I did just that—I slept for a week; then I was fine, I *thought*.

As the years passed, I became progressively addicted to coffee, cigarettes and booze. Another step in my "gradual" slip downward took place one evening during my fifth pregnancy.

That night I decided to sit home with my husband and have a martini instead of going to the church meeting. That was the beginning of a change in priorities. Before that time, I would only drink when we went out on dates. This was the first time I chose to sit down to relax and have a drink instead of keeping my previous commitment to attend a meeting.

After that it took about seven years before my priorities degenerated from relaxing with a drink one night a week, to a lifestyle consisting of parties, until we had "one" *big* party which seemed to last all summer. Eventually booze wasn't enough to satisfy my cravings, and I "graduated" to marijuana.

Deception

The formerly naive, sweet, prudish Nancy began living in the fast lane. I even started smoking cigarettes at age thirty-four. I was becoming everything I judged my mother to be, and worse.

The pictures taken of me at that time captured the stoned look on my face, showing how deceived I had become. At the time, I thought I looked great. In fact, I did what was typical of most people "hooked" during the early seventies culture. Despite being the mother of five children, I looked down on the values' system of my Catholic upbringing and said, "That stuff is nuts. I am now enlightened. I don't have to live by these codes and guidelines. I am free."

Raised as a devout Catholic, my life had been surrounded by some positive influences that were focused on God. Before my moral degeneration, I usually had good pastors to help me through each crisis. But with the influence of the seventies culture, I thought I was full of wisdom with all that "self" stuff. *What deception!*

Now that I look back I can see clearly the demonic influence creeping into our family. Not only did alcoholism have a stronghold on us because we were not aware that "drinking problems" ran in families, but it was also perpetuated because of the great *secrecy conspiracy.* No one was willing to admit its existence. In addition, we were being pulled into a downward spiral by the culture around us.

CHAPTER SEVEN

The Curse of the Occult

I grew up with a love for music, especially the great classics. The man I married also had a collection of classical music. Beginning with my trombone playing, music had the capability of having a profound influence on me. Well, somehow our taste in music started changing.

Along with many other Americans, we were influenced by the rock and drug music. Eastern mysticism was laced throughout much of it. Then there was the play, *Hair*. We went to Coconut Grove in Miami and saw it live. Because I went after consuming several drinks, I had no resistance to the demonic spirits operating in that theater. A different person walked out of there, one who now believed the whole Judeo-Christian ethic was stupid. The message of that play had more power than the words that were spoken or the music that was played.

The devil took advantage of me through one of my greatest gifts and areas of sensitivity, music. I have since learned a major truth from that experience: *A sober person who has not short-circuited his will with anesthetic can maintain his value system or return to it after a short sojourn into sin. A drunk goes only one direction—into more destruction.*

After that, I no longer believed there was sin or evil or judgment. I bought into bondage and thought it was freedom. Involvement in a transactional analysis training group further demolished my sense of responsibility to my family. I was preoccupied with curiosity about "what makes me tick."

Along with that, we were dabbling in the occult at our parties. (Remember, I said one of the causes for a curse is involvement in the occult.)

One friend was into astrology and reincarnation, another into yoga, and we tried mind reading and water witching. If we had known what we were doing, we wouldn't have done it; but the Bible was foreign to us and we didn't know of God's warnings.

Caught in Satan's Trap

Carrying the negative occultic influences, I experienced two traumatic events which totally changed the culture of our family. The first was my dad's death. While I attended his funeral I had missed some meetings that were required by our church. The second blow came when a cold-hearted pastor refused to let my daughter receive her First Communion with her class as a result of the missed meetings. The rejection was too painful— we walked away from our church and away from God. There would be nowhere else to turn when the next inevitable crisis arrived.

During this period I broke my tailbone, broke my toes

several times, had severe migraine headaches and began to see the children as an interference in my lifestyle.

When we had company I would tell the children, "Go and make yourself invisible." I was doing the very thing I had resented so much when my mom was sick or too preoccupied for me. Eventually, our occultic participation began reaping grim consequences.

Nightmare

One night I had a horrible nightmare. In it I had an uncontrollable urge to go into the kitchen, get a butcher knife and stab all five children. In the dream, while on my way to get the knife, I had stopped in the hallway to change the temperature on the thermostat.

A deep, frightening shudder of shock registered throughout my body when I woke up from the dream and found myself actually standing in the hallway changing the thermostat. I was, in reality, on my way to get the knife.

Almost as startling, the next day one of the children told me he had a very strange dream the night before. He related that *he had dreamed I had a knife and was going to stab all the children!*

Had some sinister unseen force directed these events? *Were there demons affecting our life?*

During this same cynical period of "motherhood burnout," I had another experience which all mothers dread: *the phone call.*

The voice on the other end of the line sounded urgent. A man asked for me and told me that my sixteen-year-old son had been bitten by a large water moccasin.

"Would you like me to take your boy to the hospital?" he asked with alarming caution.

"Yes, of course," I answered, feeling little emotion.

71

My child was in the emergency room, already delirious from the venom when I arrived. The doctors were discussing his treatment, but they were not in agreement about what to do. There was evident concern, not only for his life, but for the possibility that he could lose his hand or arm.

The next several days my boy was in a hospital bed with his arm all black from the snakebite. I hardly remember my visits to his room, but I remember feeling no emotion. It wasn't the result of shock; I was burned out. (Praise the Lord, he recovered completely.)

Why no emotions? You see, there had been so many medical emergencies and accidents over the years that I no longer reacted. There had been the febrile convulsions, hernias, tonsils, meningitis, tumors, falls on heads, fall-off-top-of-high-dive on head, speech therapy and allergies. Later on there were about a dozen auto accidents.

Suicide

During those "Supermom" years I was constantly tired and short on time. I didn't have the energy to finish the chores that I had started. There were days when I would mow our half-acre of lawn with a self-propelled mower, a mother's day gift. While my husband golfed one Saturday, I repainted our battered station wagon with a one-inch wide paintbrush and Rust-Oleum. I was constantly driving the children to their activities at separate locations and then returning to pick them up, not to speak of the cooking, cleaning and laundry for seven.

One evening when I became enraged about my unfair workload, I lashed out at my husband and started packing suitcases. I had already had a few drinks, and my mind was fogged.

Believing there was no way out, feeling totally unappreciated, I grabbed my purse in the middle of the fight with my husband and stormed out the door. *This is it. I'll end my miserable life. Maybe then someone will appreciate me.*

I can still see the dark road in my mind's eye as I drove recklessly past the orange groves to my destruction. Sobbing hysterically, I aimed the car toward a telephone pole, poised to "floor" the accelerator.

I have no explanation for what happened next, except that God must have sent an angel to prevent my self-destruction. When I proceeded to stomp on the gas pedal, my foot, instead, *hit the brakes!*

I have no memory of what happened next.

Alcohol blocks the resolution of emotional problems and crises. That is why the addict fails to *mature or develop character* as a result of "valley" experiences.

Wounded Children

While all this turmoil encompassed our lives, I had no idea that I was emotionally destroying the children.

A typical night in our home consisted of me sitting in a beanbag chair in our living room. The only other furniture consisted of another large, velvet beanbag like the one upon which I sat, two small beanbag chairs, an aquarium, a super stereo system and ash trays. Completing the decor was a red-and-blue, four-inch-shag carpet that had to be raked now and then.

Our evenings started out with several martini's, a bottle of wine and a couple of black Russians after dinner. Sometimes we would drink until it was almost dawn. In all of that I had *absolutely no idea how much my family culture and I had changed,* nor how traumatic this was for our children.

All this transpired despite my adamant decision as a young girl **never to repeat the horrible mistakes my mother made.** My children's lives were being damaged in worse ways than mine had been, but I was unaware and helpless to make the necessary changes at that time. Had there been any awareness on my part, I could have seen the patterns that emerged in my offspring:

(1) Two of them were bed-wetters like I had been. I wasn't able to provide the loving and secure environment that I so desperately wanted to give them.

(2) Then there were all the accidents. They plagued me just as they had seemed to follow my parents, then the children were affected.

(3) The children also experienced rejection from me, just as I had received from my mother.

One time when I was still smoking secretly, I broke a promise to my daughter because of that addiction. I had told her that we would go shopping together to a large mall in another town. She was so excited about going shopping alone with me, which was rare in a family with five children. While getting ready for the excursion, I realized that if she was with me I couldn't smoke without exposing my deception. So I drove off alone, leaving her crying in the driveway.

God's Hand on Their Lives

My children were given talents by God to help them get through their crises, just as music had been the remedy that had helped me survive.

For one son it was golf. His love of the game kept him disciplined and occupied with winning tournaments while our home life was disintegrating. If he wasn't a talented and dedicated athlete, he probably would have been a high school dropout. He was awarded a college scholarship.

Some of the children received great healing and deliverance from the Lord, but that was not to come until later. In the meantime, I continued to exhibit all the characteristics of an adult child of an alcoholic *(see page 199 for a complete list of these)* without even recognizing it.

As a result of this behavior which ruled my life, I wasn't able to be a good wife like I wanted to be, and our family continued to deteriorate until we were hit with the greatest tragedy of all.

My husband divorced me, leaving me alone to care for five children.

PART II:

Recognizing and Growing:
The Discovery Phase

CHAPTER EIGHT

Discovery!
New Hope at Last

D *ivorce.* It was the last thing that I ever dreamed could happen to me. Twenty years of marriage came to a sudden, painful end.

Suddenly, I was alone, a nursing student with five children ages eleven to eighteen years, in a situation that I could not control at all.

The children were deeply wounded as well. My oldest son was the first to react. He had been awarded a college scholarship; but his dad left me right after school started, and the news devastated him. After several weeks of turmoil, he joined the army, and later wrote this:

"The experience which changed my life the most would have to be my parent's divorce. It all happened my freshman year of college, while going to Brevard. This was 1978 and I was eighteen—my first time away from home. I called home one day and asked to speak to my dad.

"My little brother said, 'Dad doesn't live here anymore.'

"I told him to stop kidding and get Dad. Well, I found out he wasn't kidding. I was in shock, so I got my dad's phone number and called him up. He tried to explain, but I could not understand.

"I stayed in bed for a week and then dropped out of school and joined the army. I was just trying to escape reality. We had always been a close family, or so I thought. In the army I grew up a little and began to understand what happened. It took me two years to finally forgive my parents. When I left the service I met my new step-parents and talked to my real ones...."

Each of the other children experienced the trauma of divorce in a different way, while I tried to cope by using the old methods I had learned. I jogged more and started entering races, developed better nutritional habits and attempted to get lost in music. Then I tried education, and finally, the classic escape, drinking.

Nothing worked. Nothing brought peace. Nothing gave me any answers.

I was feeling helpless and had run out of all hope, until one morning during a run when I called out to God. As I returned home to read the paper, it was as if God directed me to a page of the newspaper that I never paid attention to before.

A list of announcements in small print called my attention to a group meeting for divorcing and separated adults. I went. There it was suggested that I get alone by myself and finally face the situation.

With much apprehension I drove myself to the beach, checked into a motel and fearfully waited for 'something' to happen. Perhaps I would receive some great insight.

The first night was uneventful—I spent it locked in my room with my cooler full of health foods and wine. As I sat on the edge of the bed the next morning tying my running shoes, I flipped the TV for something other than cartoons. My eye caught a program featuring a man who was a runner like me. He was talking about Jesus.

This man was a member of the Fellowship of Christian Athletes and he was telling me, another runner, the plan of salvation.

His simple gospel narrative amazed me, having been raised a Catholic. It seemed too simple—*could it be true that all I had to do was give my messed up life to Jesus Christ?...just ask Him into my heart, tell Him I was sorry for my sins, and make Him Lord of my life?*

I decided to consider doing that. *After all, what could I lose?*

While running my second mile on the beach, I finally gave up and said something like this: *"Well, God, I've made a mess of my life and don't know how to fix it. I'm sorry for my sins. Will You take my life? I believe You can restore it, so I ask You Jesus to come into my heart right now. Amen."*

Wow! Peace suddenly flooded through me and I experienced the meaning of Philippians 4:7: "And the peace of God, which transcends all understanding, will guard your hearts and your minds in Christ Jesus."

Almost immediately after that, while I was still running, God gave me some specific instructions. He knew that I dreaded this first, lonely Christmas which was quickly approaching. The Lord's guidance was twofold: to invite, and to go. He told me to invite my family to our house Christmas Eve. Next, He instructed me to take the children to Miami on Christmas day to be with old friends who would be a comfort to us.

After receiving my "orders" I celebrated my new life with Jesus in a unique "ceremony" of joy.

As I sat in the sand watching a nearby group parasailing, a sudden vital awareness overcame me. I no longer had to watch and wish—I had new courage to participate.

So in the first minutes of new life I experienced the exhileration of being towed by a boat and flying through the air.

I soared unencumbered above the beautiful coast of Sarasota, Florida, as free as the newborn spirit within me, just released from thirty-eight years of bondage.

Exhilarating! It was my unique way to enjoy the beauty of God's creation and celebrate His new life in Jesus.

First Christian Assignment

"And we know that in all things God works for the good of those who love him, who have been called according to his purpose" (Romans 8:28).

That first scripture I memorized after I was born again proved to be true for the children and me as I launched into my new life with Jesus.

My first task as a new Christian, as I said, was to share God's love on Christmas Eve. I invited my mom, my brother, his wife, their five children and their grandparents. We had a wonderful Christmas Eve dinner and evening together.

Then God protected us all from having to face loneliness the next day. We packed and left the house early on Christmas morning and spent three days with good friends the children had grown up with. Keeping busy like that prevented depression from ruining that holiday season. God's wisdom, I would continue to discover, is far beyond any wisdom of man.

Enthusiasm

Because I was so excited about my salvation, I talked about Jesus and my newfound peace almost everywhere

I went. Everyone listened tolerantly and, surprisingly, they all continued to be friendly: Mom, my brother and my friends. Only my psychology instructor criticized me—and that was for not taking credit and praising myself.

I experienced one major failure, however. I feel it is important to share this failure so that you can see how God gives us more chances.

After my husband left me, I went through "hell" until I was saved. The instructors at the community college watched me enter nursing school full of enthusiasm, had seen me devastated by divorce, and then realized that I was suddenly full of joy.

Normally nursing students from our school who experienced divorce failed or dropped out of school. But I was arriving at class every day in a great mood and getting good grades.

So six months after my husband left me, and three months after my salvation, I was approached and asked to speak at a special "Seminar on Success" which featured people who had survived a major life crisis. They asked me to share what methods I used to cope with divorce. I wanted to do it, but I was scared half-to-death.

When my turn arrived to speak, I lost my nerve after hearing the other speakers share their secular solutions. As an ACoA (although I didn't know that I was at that time), I couldn't face the possibility of being rejected for talking about Jesus Christ. I didn't even mention Him.

I'd like to say that ever since I was a Christian all I ever did was brag on Him. But despite what Jesus had done for me, I didn't have the guts to tell about Him to an audience searching for answers.

This embarrassing story is one that I have never before admitted to in public. I include it because it is possible that if I lost my nerve and kept my Christianity hidden, you may have done the same thing, or may be tempted to. Don't let the devil harass you and condemn you. God forgave me and He will forgive you and give you more opportunities to share what He is doing in your life. As you get free from bondage to the addictions which contaminate your life, the boldness will come.

Taking Off the Old

I began witnessing for Christ a great deal, but because I was such a new Christian I didn't have any teaching. I was still drinking and wasn't studying the Bible. I had not found a church to attend yet, because I was saved through a television ministry.

I was a "new creature" according to the Bible and in God's eyes: "Therefore, if anyone is in Christ, he is a new creation; the old has gone, the new has come" (2 Corinthians 5:17). But there was still enough of the old nature evident to maintain sick relationships.

"I do not understand what I do. For what I want to do I do not do, but what I hate I do. And if I do what I do not want to do, I agree that the law is good. As it is, it is no longer I myself who do it, but it is sin living in me. I know that nothing good lives in me, that is, in my sinful nature. For I have the desire to do what is good, but I cannot carry it out. For what I do is not the good I want to do; no, the evil I do not want to do—this I keep on doing. Now if I do what I do not want to do, it is no longer I who do it, but it is sin living in me that does it.

"So I find this law at work: When I want to do good, evil is right there with me. For in my inner being I delight in God's law; but I see another law at work in the members of my body, waging war against the law of my mind and making me a prisoner of the law of sin at work within my members. What a wretched man I am! Who will rescue me from this body of death? Thanks be to God—through Jesus Christ our Lord!" (Romans 7:15-25).

Ken

While I was still struggling to find who I was in Christ, I met Ken. Both of us had been born again about three months. After his conversion Ken realized that after a divorce and ten years of single life, God was preparing him to have a wife.

So, at the time we met, Ken was praying for "a woman who could golf, beat him at tennis and who loved Jesus." He was so serious in his pursuit of a wife that he had been flying women to his home for a week at a time. There he would have his children evaluate her during a home-cooked meal—he is a great pressure cooker chef— then he would take her to church on Sunday. So far all of those women had failed the "church test" that Ken required.

We met at a Parents Without Partners party. It was a "bring-your-own-bottle party" where everyone brought their own liquor and snacks.

When Ken walked in the door wearing a white turtleneck shirt and a blue sportcoat, his dark brown hair, full white beard and twinkling eyes immediately caught my attention.

He was carrying two grocery bags containing a blender, orange juice, ice cream, vodka, and giant cups. He then proceeded to mix drinks and share them with the women. He was the only unselfish man at the party and *I wanted to meet him!*

He wasted no time in getting to the point. "Do you golf?" he asked.

"Yes."

"Do you play tennis?"

"Of course."

Then he slipped in the clincher: "Do you love Jesus?"

"Yes!" I was thrilled to answer.

As we dated we played tennis almost every night. A funny thing happened, though. Ken could not beat me at a single set of tennis for an entire year! Sometimes a set would be five to two in his favor, but I always ended up winning.

When I reminded him of his plea to God for a woman who could beat him at tennis, he talked to God about that matter, and from then on we played about even.

Still babes in Christ, it was fifteen months after we started living together that we attended a church pastored by Karl Strader. During that service Ken felt convicted regarding our lifestyle. We came home and he called and invited the children to the wedding, and we married ten days after that sermon.

Sobriety

One day, after four months in our new church home, now called the Carpenter's Home Church, Pastor Strader's teaching gave us increasing clarity and direction. Ken and I began to understand that drinking was not to be a part of our Christian lives. We wanted to get involved in church activities and to join the church, but the little instruction book they gave us said that members of the Assembly of God church were not to smoke or drink.

That did it. We were starting new lives together, and we wanted to *belong*. The booze was thrown out. The following Saturday when we went to another party with our same group of friends, we took our own root beer and diet cokes.

WE WERE NEVER INVITED BACK TO ANOTHER OF THEIR GATHERINGS AGAIN, AND NONE OF THEM EVER ACCEPTED ANY OF OUR INVITATIONS EITHER.

I couldn't understand it. I called, I wrote out invitations and I asked them over for dinner or to our new Bible study on Friday nights. No response. It was over.

Conviction!

The end of a marriage of almost twenty years duration didn't cause my old friends to avoid me. In fact, during the trying times of grief and turmoil, my peers and family stood by my side and offered comfort and support.

Even remarriage didn't destroy those relationships. Everyone seemed to accept Ken, and it was parties as usual—even though Ken taught a singles Sunday School class. He took two of my children and me to church, and we were reading the Bible together.

My becoming a Christian didn't drive them away either. (Ken and I weren't able to understand, though, why we couldn't convert anyone to Christ.)

We had what we called our "barroom ministry." Over wine or cocktails we would talk about how wonderful Jesus was and why others should give their lives to Him. No results. We didn't know why, since Christianity had so obviously changed our lives—or so we thought. But we weren't doing the following; therefore, we were ineffective.

"For this very reason, make every effort to add to your faith goodness; and to goodness, knowledge; and to knowledge, self-control; and to self-control, perseverance; and to perseverance, godliness; and to godliness, brotherly kindness; and to brotherly kindness, love. For if you possess these qualities in increasing measure, they will keep you from being ineffective and unproductive in your knowledge of our Lord Jesus Christ. But if anyone does not have them, he is nearsighted and blind, and has forgotten that he has been cleansed from his past sins'' (2 Peter 1:5-9).

As far as I know, all those friendships ended when there was an obvious, outward change in our lives which reflected what Christ had recreated inwardly.

What *was* the change that made the difference in old relationships? ***Sobriety.***

Being sober meant that I really had changed...really had become a Christian...really was a *new creature* in Christ. Possibly my sobriety convicted our old friends of their own sins, and it was too uncomfortable for them. From that point on we were totally alienated from their lives.

Reformed Drunk

''There's nothing worse than a reformed drunk.'' I grew up hearing that. Former drinkers were the target of the most degrading statements made among my parents and their peers. Later in life I was to hear that statement again, and even say it myself.

Why?

Through natural eyes, drinkers (and other addicts) see former drinkers (and addicts) as traitors; self-righteous, arrogant, and judgmental.

What does a ''reformed drunk'' usually do to incur the wrath of his old friends? He tries to convert those who are still in bondage to the stuff.

Even if the former addict doesn't actually confront his friends and loved ones with the reality of their drinking problems, the former addict's new lifestyle, behavior, and attitude arouse feelings of condemnation in them.

I know, because for a season I lost my relationship (even though they were sick ones) with my mom, brother and every single friend that I had made over a twenty-year period.

How? By getting sober. During my lifetime there were many other catastrophes that put strains on relationships, but those crises didn't destroy them. In fact, family and friends stood by me during those periods of adjustment—until I became sober.

Even though I was rejected, that didn't keep me from trying. I would visit my brother and tell him how wonderful it was to wake up every morning feeling good—how neat it was to look forward to each day, not just party nights. I offered to pray for him and help him be set free of the compulsion to drink. He denied he had a problem and stopped inviting me or our family to his home. That was sad because his five children and my five had grown up together. Now the cousins were destined to become strangers.

I've learned since that a drinker is miserable at non-drinking functions and avoids them. In fact, looking back, I remember that in all our travels and vacations every restaurant we chose served cocktails.

Nothing worse than a reformed drunk? Absolutely—to a drinker. The Bible explains why:

"Why do you look at the speck of sawdust in your brother's eye and pay no attention to the plank in your own eye? How can you say to your brother, 'Let me take the speck out of your eye,' when all the time there is a plank in your own eye? You hypocrite, first take the plank out of your own eye, and then you will see clearly to remove the speck from your brother's eye" (Matthew 7:3-5).

This is what really happens. If the devil couldn't keep us (addicts) from getting saved, he then pushes us to hurry up and try to fix everyone else right away.

That doesn't work because our own eyes are full of planks: pride, fears, lust, bitterness, confusion, insecurity, etc. Those we are in such a hurry to help see this junk. We run too quickly, attempting to restore others lives before our own is restored— and we head ourselves toward frustration, loneliness and burnout.

Even Saint Paul waited three years after his conversion before he began preaching the good news, the gospel (Galatians 1:17-18).

The mistake I made is being repeated all over creation: "I've found the answer and I want you to have the same great experience I've had." To others it doesn't appear that "great," because they can see all the contamination remaining in our lives.

The Word tells us to get the planks out of our own eyes first, and then we can see clearly to get the specks out of theirs. It seems that God is advising us to *slow down*. We can drop that role we picked up as children— we don't have to do it all yesterday!

Let us get our lives and emotions restored first. Then those who still need help will see the fruit of the Holy Spirit radiating in our lives. They'll see love, joy, peace, patience, kindness, goodness, faithfulness, gentleness, and self-control (Galatian 5:22). They are more likely to want what we've found after our inner man is renewed.

How?

There is only one power capable of changing the inner man. That is the power of God through prayer. And I don't mean "now I lay me down to sleep" prayers. I'm talking about spiritual warfare prayer, New Testament style:

"All the people were amazed and said to each other,

'What is this teaching? With authority and power he gives orders to evil spirits and they come out!' '' (Luke 4:36).

One of the ways to get to the point of release from the contamination of our past is through the ministry of deliverance, or the casting out of evil spirits. It is a demonic force that produces ungodly fruit (sinful behavior) in our lives.

For example, my husband, Ken, had a problem with cursing. He loved Jesus with all his heart, but when he was under pressure he would curse. His language embarrassed us. One day while golfing with a young minister, he happened to hit a bad slice and it landed in the water. This was a brand new golf ball, so in his frustration he uttered an obscenity. Then he teed up another new ball, hit it into the water and again cursed. After the third ball was drowned, the same verbal reaction followed. Pastor Ron said, "Ken, do you want to swear like that?"

Ken answered, "No, I sure don't."

So Ron laid his hands on Ken's head and said, "You spirit of blasphemy, *go in the name of Jesus!*" Ken laughed for a few seconds, and *with that breath* the demon that caused Ken to curse left him.

When he returned home from golfing he came without that language. He no longer had to try to suppress it; he no longer had to squelch the desire to swear. The urge to curse was no longer in him! That is what happens when a person gets delivered from a demon. It doesn't matter if it is a demon of fear, anxiety, lust or *alcoholism*. The name of Jesus is above all other names. The Lord wants you to be equipped to deal with these things, which is why I wrote this book.

Increasing Wisdom

Our first year as new Christians had taught us a great

deal. Ken and I were learning more about our relationship with Jesus and the spiritual realm. We also began to understand why our old friends had turned away.

We had becomed reformed drunks—intolerable for two reasons:

(1) We were trying to fix others before we were restored ourselves and the others saw all our faults.

(2) We had finally found victory over old fears, insecurities and bad attitudes, and our presence among the addicts made them miserable. Their eventual response was inevitably one of these:

(a) They would avoid us in order to avoid facing the fact that they needed to change—**Denial!**

(b) Eventually they will see that we are "real" and seek help so they can be happy too.

CHAPTER NINE

Searching for Normal

Pain is a strange tutor, but it was out of a tearful encounter with my mother that I learned to how to say, "I'm sorry." Applying that simple principle produced more healing in my relationships with my own children than any other.

The more restoration I received, the greater was my desire to bring that same healing to those I loved most. My heart began to turn toward my children as I called out to God for their restoration. Almost a year after I "learned" to apologize, I traveled to see each of my five children and find out in what ways I had hurt them. As each painful episode unfolded, I asked for their forgiveness.

One of my sons shared that he was most hurt when he was in Junior High, and we made him change schools. He said it devastated him. When that decision was made, I had no idea that it would hurt him so badly—that is how the devil used me to try to destroy him, and I was unaware of it. We made that decision to change his school while we were drinking with our friends, and the drinking numbed my sensitivity to his potential pain.

Divorce was the focal point of pain for my youngest son. He wrote this poem when he was a senior in high school, six years after the divorce:

A Not Too Long Before Ago

a not too long before ago
i felt as cold as winter snow
GODISNOWHERE as i do recall
to ease the pain and stop the fall

so we've held up high our
heads so
low
and tried to shun the
winter snow

but man in all his in(finite) knowledge
does not know and can not show
what so low we held up high

Dearly beloved we are gathered
(under no true commitment)

to say i do but mean i
don't bother

'cause in a while it's all over
families fall apart and out
dreams die children cry
when we decide in our mortal
(soul)

—no longer can i feel the love

so if i die before i wake
i know it's not a big mistake

When this poem was published in the high school book of art and short stories, my son asked me to read it. Because I was still suffering myself from the scars of rejection, I didn't feel any emotion.

This poem is a cry for help and understanding, and my son reached out for understanding and healing from his pain, but I didn't respond at all. Can you imagine how he felt? Can you see how dysfunctional patterns can continue for generations without God's intervention?

Four years later, after God healed me and restored my emotions, I discovered this poem while cleaning one day.

It made me cry.

At last I was able to weep for my young son's pain and to pray for his release.

Motorcycle Mama

God dealt in an unusual way with one daughter. Her healing resulted from a motorcycle ride—one of the more "adventuresome" chapters in my life!

While my oldest son was stationed in Germany, he golfed in all the European tournaments he could enter. He won so many that the Army was sending him to a base in Maryland to play in the All-Army, -Navy, -Air Force, and -Marine Tournament.

Ken and I were still newlyweds with plenty of financial struggles; so we rode motorcycles. I had been riding only six months when the news came that my son would be coming back to the states for the golf tournament. I wanted to see him.

So on a Saturday night the decision was made that my nineteen-year-old daughter and I would ride on my Suzuki 450 to Maryland, camping along the way. Sunday morning our pastor prayed for our safety, and that afternoon we left. I remember telling Ken that if I could navigate that difficult corner a mile from our home, the motorcycle loaded high with sleeping bags, tents, peanut butter, instant tea and pickles, then we would go all the way. If not, we would return home. We made the first corner and kept right on going.

What a trip! The motorcycle had fallen over on our driveway before we left and soaked our tuna sandwiches with gasoline. They sure tasted funny, but I couldn't tell what was wrong because we had been on the highway smelling car exhaust all day.

Camping the first night was fun, and by the next day we made it to the outskirts of Washington, D.C. I had never been north of North Carolina, so riding on the interstate through the cities and traffic was a challenging experience, to say the least.

OOPS!

The day we were to see my son we broke camp and headed north again. At 9:15 a.m. we were on the Washington Beltway in rush hour traffic—two women with sleeping bags and tents dangling off the back sissy bar of our little red Suzuki. Suddenly we started sliding around. It felt like we hit butter. I hollered, "Honey, stop wiggling!"

She replied, "I'm not wiggling." Then I realized that the rear tire had blown out.

"Now what do I do?" I looked at my rear-view mirror and saw that the lane on my left was clear, so I headed for the grass, shouting to my daughter to put her feet on the ground as soon as I stopped.

Ken had given us each a mace gun in case of any emergencies. I thought we were going to need them when I saw the neighborhood we had stopped near. My daughter laid on the grass, and I prayed for help. Within five minutes two police cars had stopped and one radioed for help. Five minutes later he returned to describe the truck that was coming to help us, so we wouldn't be misled by someone else.

I was certainly glad he did that, because when our rescuers came in two trucks, they looked tough, and I would have run down the highway if the officer hadn't described their vehicles. It turned out that they were very kind. They strapped my motorcycle in a sleeping bag so it wouldn't get scratched and hoisted it up onto the truck. Then they drove us to the repair place and even took us to MacDonald's for breakfast.

After the tire was fixed we hopped back on and headed for the golf course. My son was a little worried because we were late, but we had a great reunion. He didn't make the cut for the team, but we all had two super days together. It was so great to see my son doing so well after all he had been through.

Not Again!

We started on our way home when on the bridge from Washington, D.C. to Virginia, again in rush hour traffic, I suddenly felt my bike skid and heard pinging sounds. We were surrounded by traffic, and the bike was handling funny. The metal clanging sound caused alarm and instinctively I tested my brake.

I had no rear brake. The metal rod that was broken was bounding off the pavement and hitting the bike. The end of the bridge was still one-fourth of a mile away and I knew I had to get there and stop somehow. If I used the front brake at the speed I was going, we would flip over the handlebars. So I downshifted for the first time in my life, and we started slowing down.

Meanwhile, my daughter was holding out her hand to

signal the traffic to slow down and watch out for us. We made it to the end of the bridge and safely stopped, using the front brake. As the cars and trucks passed us, I could tell that a miracle had happened, because they were bunched up just inches apart from each other. No one hit us and no one piled up into each other. I could almost see the angels acting as bumpers between the vehicles.

I took out my tool kit and took apart the brake assembly. What had happened? The repair man had forgotten to put the cotter pin back into the brake assembly and it came apart. When the metal part rotated, it pressed on the brake rod and broke it.

At the rest stop up the highway we called a repair shop in the next town. They came and got us. That afternoon we slept in one of the boats they had on display in the parking lot, even though it was raining on us—we were worn out.

God's Purpose

How was all this adventure affecting my daughter? She saw how God had intervened and kept us safe through thunderstorms, blowouts and other disasters. Because she experienced safety where there should have been calamity, she went to church two weeks later and **gave her life to Jesus Christ**.

So, God had plans that were beyond a reunion with a son. He was preparing my daughter's heart to be open to Him.

Guessing at Normal

At the same time God was healing my children, He was doing a complete "workover" on me!

Adult children of alcoholics guess at what normal is, so while I was floundering to find "normal," the changes taking place in my heart were being reflected by the transformation in my closet. In the beginning of my Christian walk I rode a motorcycle, wore slacks or blue jeans with plaid shirts, and arrived at church with boots on my feet and a helmet in my hand. I honestly believed that I was just what that church needed.

Eventually the blue jeans and motorcycle helmet made me feel out of place among the church women dressed in more traditional fashion, so I decided to study the women in church and try to figure out how they put themselves together. I also remember that I didn't feel I was worth the time it took to groom myself daily. In fact, I remember that, years ago, I used to wonder how women in the neighborhood could look pretty in the morning. I really didn't know how they did it. Now I realize that one area of training that I missed was how to be a lady. I did not enjoy typical female things like shopping, makeup or dresses. It was something I would have to learn.

To this day I can't curl my hair, although I've learned that with my facial shape I'm supposed to wear my hair straight. God really worked that one out for me. But I had to learn how to be ladylike and dress in a feminine manner. I wasn't trying to be someone I was not, I was trying to find out who I was. All I knew was that I had missed something as I grew up, and I wanted to be all that God had created me to be. I didn't know then about the defense mechanisms and roles that I had acquired in order to survive. I only knew that I had not been happy. God took care of my new training program.

A New Creature

During that time of searching for guidance and a new map for my life, I devoured the Bible. In my first year with the Lord I put away all the *Time* magazines, nursing journals and newspapers, and read nothing but the Bible.

I took notes in all of the church services. Joyce Strader, my pastors wife, said during one of our radio interviews, that she had observed me taking notes in church and thought it was unusual. I had assumed everyone took notes, because the explanation of the Bible was so exciting!

God directed me to replace the contaminations of the past—humanism, New Age thinking, etc., with His Word only—not interpretations of His Word, but just His Word. Now, even though I read other things, I don't have a strong desire to do so. I do it because I believe it's necessary to know a little of what is going on in life for those who come for help, for example, what's new in medicine or what's happening concerning the abortion issue. When an issue is being featured by the media it affects those to whom we are ministering.

Most important, just like the Word restored me, the Word is the backbone of all other restoration also, including yours. If we know the real thing, we will be able to recognize the counterfeits also.

Tomboy

It is possible that my parents expected a boy before I was born, which may have added to my confusion in identities. I am the firstborn. I've never questioned my mother about it because I was unable to communicate with her on that level. All the memories of my young life are "Nancy is a tomboy," and "Jack-of-all-trades, master of none." God has now turned that into a blessing, because I can do things that I wouldn't have been able to do without my background.

One day in the North Carolina mountains, our son-in-law and Ken decided to cut down some trees on our property. When one fell across the road blocking vehicular traffic, I picked up the chainsaw, started it and cut the tree trunk into manageable pieces while the men moved them out of the way.

My Closet

Back to the wardrobe: I wanted to look the way I felt as God was bringing me down the path He had for me, but I didn't know what to do or how to do it.

The high school I went to used uniforms. I didn't learn how to put on makeup, and never learned how to shop for a wardrobe.

So when I gave my life to Jesus at age thirty-eight, my only prior experience in dressing up was for church or a party. I often looked like a clown. The old pictures verify that. It's funny, but I felt and looked older at age thirty than I do now at almost age fifty. Even my children tell me this. **God can restore your life this way, too**.

I didn't know how to make myself look like a woman. So as a new Christian I decided the best way was to look around at my new environment—at the singers in church and at the other women. I didn't think I could look like any of them, because my image of myself was very poor, even though I had a new husband who loved me, and I was seeing God turn my children's lives around.

I needed something in addition to being saved, delivered and turned around; I needed teaching and training. God sent a precious woman across my path who taught me how to wear makeup and in what kind of clothes I would look best. After the colorful transformation of my face people actually stopped me in the aisles of the supermarket and told me how wonderful I looked.

Once my closet was filled with jeans, t-shirts, and tie-dyed tops. Then, as my quest for wholeness continued, I added tennis outfits, jogging clothes and shoes, and a black gown for symphony concerts. With the motorcycle came boots, helmet and a windbreaker.

Finally came my sojourn into skirts, pantyhose, high heels and jewelry. Now, after ten years with Jesus, I am in a church leadership position. I have clothes for TV and teaching seminars, and I feel confident when I dress, thanks to the people God sent to teach me how.

What We See Now

On a regular basis, we see similar needs after we minister to others.

An obese person needs retraining in nutrition, shopping and cooking after his or her deliverance.

A person set free from homosexuality may need re-education in dressing, mannerisms and speech.

Poverty leaves people without any skills for managing money. They need financial counsel after Jesus sets them free.

Former addicts need communication skills, leadership skills and training in a host of other areas. If a person "dropped out" through addiction at age eighteen and became sober at age thirtyeight, he is still eighteen emotionally, and now has to "grow up."

That is why Spiritual Warfare Ministries calls deliverance a spiritual "Chapter XI." The demons are off your back, and you have time and peace to get your act together.

CHAPTER TEN

Hazel the Bear

We woke up that morning to a phone call. "Hazel the bear has escaped. Have you heard it on the news?"

It looked like our new marriage was definitely off to an exciting start. When we listened to the radio, as we were dressing, we heard that a bear had escaped at the Masterpiece Gardens tourist attraction in Lake Wales, Florida and the tourists were holed up in the gift shop.

So we hopped onto our motorcycles and zoomed to Lake Wales, as we had been doing every day. Only this time we were headed toward an extraordinary day. The adrenalin was surging.

Many thoughts raced through my head as I quietly rode behind Ken's motorcycle those thirty-five miles.

I had believed when I married Ken three months earlier that "now we would have a nice, quiet, stable, low-key, mature and relaxing life together." It is amazing how persuasive the spirit of denial can be. I was holding that belief despite of all the "symptoms" in our lives and the lives of our eight children.

I didn't understand how much our relationship was contingent on my programming to be a "rescuer" and a "crisis-dependent" person.

When we met, it was because Ken had asked God to send him a Christian woman who could golf, beat him at tennis and who loved Jesus. We played tennis almost nightly during our fifteen-month courtship. I saw only the fun part of our relationship. On the other hand, I was blind to all of Ken's problems, and he had lots of them!

Problems

Ken's tourist attraction, Masterpiece Gardens, was founded by his dad who had purchased the beautiful mosaic of Leonardo da Vinci's *Last Supper*. The attraction was in a Chapter XI bankruptcy. He also was losing his house because of the financial situation. His children had problems as a result of growing up, like mine did, in a dysfunctional family.

Ken had been divorced for ten years when I met him, and he had custody of his three children. They started working at the tourist attraction when they were little—doing bird shows (he had the first trained duck show in the state of Florida), helping with train tours, ushering the tourists safely onto the skyride and operating the snack bar.

At one time the "Great Masterpiece" was one of the big three attractions in Florida. In those days (before Disney) it was Cypress Gardens, Masterpiece Gardens, and Silver Springs. Then the interstate system came in and with it another big blow, Disney World, now the Magic Kingdom. The gas shortage in the late seventies dealt the crushing blow—Ken couldn't stay above water.

As I rode toward the "bear crisis" that morning, I was hoping that this publicity would be just what was needed to get people to notice that this pretty theme park was still on the map.

Ken had tried desperately to borrow money to pay his bills, but was refused by all the financial institutions that he had approached, even though he owned all the land and the facilities free and clear. No one would give him a loan; therefore, the Chapter XI bankruptcy.

The Vision

One morning, about two months prior to this, we both had awakened with a vision—that the attraction was to be used as a Christian camp and retirement center. We had thought we had found the answer to the financial crisis. We believed it was an answer from God and even knew where the new buildings, motel, etc., would be. So we had set out to see the vision fulfilled. The gift shop in which the tourists were presently hiding had become a Christian bookstore. We had hoped to take all the money we would make that summer and start renovating the rest of the place.

What was Hazel's escape going to do to our plans, I wondered? Very shortly we were to find out a lot more about how God's kingdom operates.

As I rode up the beautiful, winding road toward the gate I could see the helicopter hovering over the jungle. They were trying to track the bear. In the parking lot were the news reporters, television crews, sheriff's department personnel, and the Florida Game and Fish Commission. I had never seen so many important people in one place before in my life. And, sure enough, the tourists were still in the gift shop!

We were told that Hazel was last seen walking along

the edge of the lawn near the sky-ride base, and then she had disappeared into the jungle.

I went out and walked around the park to see if I could spot her. It was weird, a park with no people in it. I could hear the helicopter, the squirrel monkeys, and the macaws, but no people.

The Hunt Begins

The *Tampa Tribune* featured the escape as if it was a hostage crisis. (It happened around the time of the Iranian hostage situation.) Hazel the Bear could be seen on the front page in cartoon form, and they numbered each day they featured her: Day 1, Day 2, Day 3, etc.

The Game and Fish Commission was very unhappy with Ken and less excited about the job they had of catching the bear. They tried to trap her with raccoon snares, which she escaped. Then Hazel was seen by some neighbors near a garbage dump.

We were really praying. I didn't want anyone to get hurt. Ken had confided to me that Hazel was a very mean bear. Another park had given Hazel to him because of her bad disposition

For an adrenalin junkie, this was a perfect "fix."

Ken gave me a short course on how to handle the media and newspaper reporters. I did live programs and taped reports by phone for various radio stations that called.

There seemed to be a lot of interest in this event. I hadn't realized what a public figure Ken was until this. Even my son who was stationed in the army in Germany read about the bear escape in the army newspaper.

Prayer Power

On the second day of the bear's freedom, we were contacted by some wild boar hunters who said they had dogs that could hunt Hazel down. Meanwhile, the Game and Fish Commission had brought in their dogs. By the third day I was so concerned that I called our radio station prayer line and asked people to pray for the bear to be captured.

That day Ken and I walked along the jungle before dawn. I carried a loaded gun for the first time in my life, planning to shoot the bear if she jumped out of the jungle. I could hear the dogs barking in the distance. What an adventure!

The officers from the Game and Fish Commission were in their truck with the dogs and a gun loaded with tranquilizer darts. Then Hazel just walked out of the woods and right up to the truck and stood next to them on her hind legs. (God answers prayer.)

The officer fired his gun and the tranquilizer dart just dribbled out of the end of the muzzle. He reloaded, but by then she had taken off for the woods again, this time with the dogs on her trail.

By now I was manning the phones and giving progress reports. Suddenly the officer ran into the room and said, "Go get the vet. We got Hazel, but we need to know if we can shoot her again with more drugs. Will she wake up if we don't, or will more tranquilizers kill her?"

The decision was made—no more drugs.

Soon the procession approached the newly repaired cage. The fellows who had volunteered to help were each carrying one of Hazel's legs and Ken was holding her head. She was starting to wake up when they still had about 100 yards left to haul her, so Ken was talking softly and reassuring her that she would be OK.

Ken's Arrest

After she was back in her cage we thought the crisis

had ended. As we happily returned to our motorcycles, Ken was apprehended by the Game and Fish Commission officer in front of the Channel 13 news camera. Ken was cited on two counts of letting a bear escape and endangering the public. He was actually arrested in front of the TV camera! We were shocked.

The charges each carried a $500 fine or ninety days in jail. We couldn't face the fine or the possibility of him going to jail.

What was happening to the vision God had given us?

Actually, God was preparing this Adult Child of an Alcoholic to depend on Him. I was to understand that better later.

The thought of a trial scared me more than the loose bear had. Ken had pleaded "not guilty" to the charges because the first judge had recommended he do so. He said the Game and Fish Commission would drop the charges because the charges were ridiculous and the judge couldn't even find them in the books.

That wasn't to be, though. Why? I found out that years earlier, Ken had hundreds of squirrel monkeys loose on the grounds. Then Florida passed a law that the monkeys had to be on an island or caged—separated from the tourists. Ken couldn't catch them to do it. The officer (the same one who arrested Ken for the bear escape) said that if Ken didn't catch and cage the monkeys, he would have to shoot them. So Ken had told the officer to let him know when he was coming to shoot the monkeys, because Ken would have the press, radio and television stations there so the whole world could watch the Game Commission officer kill the monkeys. It never came to pass.

Revenge

Now, apparently, was the opportunity for revenge. Hazel had escaped and Ken was not at fault. She had chewed the chain link fence while she was in heat. There are wild bears in the surrounding woods. Now the officer from the Game and Fish Commission could get even. A trial date was set.

Without God's intervention an adrenalin junkie will create a crisis when life gets too peaceful. But the Lord showed me through what was to happen that I could experience peace instead of anxiety—even though circumstances like the trial remained the same.

God wants you to know that, too. He has provided His Word to bring answers and peace for every situation.

In desperation, before I knew what God was trying to do, I went to a prayer meeting. It was led by Joyce Strader, our pastor's wife. That morning three different people opened their Bibles to Psalm 37 and one of them helped me to understand it. (See page 29 of this book).

I realized that God was saying the evildoer would talk too much and his own words would snare him. (The meaning of Psalm 37 was interpreted to me to mean that Ken would not have to utter a word in his own defense, but his accuser would talk too much and his own words would pierce his own heart.) With this reassurance I had newfound peace and absolute *trust*. (Remember, I've said that trusting is foreign to us ACoA's, but I want you to know that you must start to trust in God's Word.) I hopped on my motorcycle and raced home to tell Ken the good news.

We opened the Bible and read Psalm 37. With confidence I told Ken that we didn't have to worry about the trial, but that he would be acquitted without having to defend himself.

The trial was still two months away and Ken wanted the protection of an attorney. So we tried to retain one. Four of them said they didn't want to tackle a "Ken Curtis vs. the State of Florida" case. Finally we found one, a criminal lawyer who was my former history teacher in nursing school.

As the date approached I felt no apprehension, even though the thought of courtrooms normally intimidated me—I had never been in one.

On the day of the trial every person that was seen before Ken was booked, handcuffed and taken to jail. They were rapists and armed robbers. What was Ken doing in a room full of felons?

The State of Florida had sent all their Game and Fish Commission officials, and they filled the front row. I sat in the fifth row next to Ken with a big grin on my face as I optimistically waited our turn. The attorneys approached me and asked me to leave the courtroom. The smile on my face made them think that I had a trick up my sleeve!

During the next two hours while I waited in the hallway I peeked so I could see Ken's accuser through a little window in the door. He spent almost two hours on the stand, using all that time to hurl charges at Ken.

But, just like God said would happen, after hearing the accusations the judge called Ken to the bench, and without Ken having to utter a word in his own defense, the judge acquitted him.

Praise the Lord!

When the newspapers approached me in the hallway after the trial, I just quoted the first lines of Psalm 37. They printed their story on the front page, starting with the Bible quote.

What does this story have to do with your life? God wants you to be reassured that He will not abandon you.

You don't have to be a veteran, a "mature," "religious" or "super-spiritual" Christian to see miracles happen. You don't have to completely understand spiritual warfare to defeat attacks of the devil.

You have the Bible, and in it are all the answers to life's problems. You can have peace even before you have been able to recognize how much of your personality is really contaminated with "coping mechanisms" that you adopted as a child in order to survive your chaotic upbringing. You have to start somewhere, just as I did, using the reassurance of the Word of God to combat fear and have "peace that passes understanding."

The Auction

A few months after the bear situation, after a curse over the property was broken through prayer, Ken realized that God wanted him out of the tourist-attraction business. So he walked through the gardens and said goodbye. Then he called an auctioneer and all the property, except the mosaic of the Last Supper, was auctioned off the following February.

At that miracle auction God returned the one million dollars that Ken had lost. Soon after, the land was purchased by the Assemblies of God, Peninsular Florida district; they are in the process of building a camp with buildings in the same locations that Ken and I had seen in our vision.

It was God's plan to have a Christian camp there, but it was not in His plan for us to run it. What we have been able to do though, is have Spiritual Warfare Training Conferences there every year—and they have attracted participants from around the world. God has made a way for Ken to return to the land that his family had owned since 1929 and use it for God's glory, so it is still in the "family."

CHAPTER ELEVEN

Returning Home

We had talked about taking a trip like this for years. Milwaukee, Wisconsin is my home town, and a Women's Aglow convention was coming up. Mom had often talked of her dream of going back home with me someday. We had lived in Florida for twenty-four years, and it looked like this was the opportunity we had been waiting for.

Because of my unrecognized need to be a hero, I had several motives for making this trip with my mom. First of all I thought it would be fun to go home after fifteen years (it had been that long since I had last visited there) and see some old friends, the house where I was raised, and our relatives. On the other hand, I really believed that the Aglow convention would be the vehicle to get Mom restored and on the road to a happy life.

So we flew "home," each of us with our own fantasy of what the week would be like.

At that time I thought Mom was still "dry" (She had

joined AA with our encouragement). I still am not sure, but when we were at the hotel she would leave the room each evening and go down to the lobby for awhile. Now as I look back I can see more clearly that she was behaving erratically, being very sneaky, typical of the behavior manifested in her former drinking days. But the spirit of denial blinded me: "God gave them a spirit of stupor, eyes so that they could not see and ears so that they could not hear, to this very day" (Romans 11:8).

As for myself, I still did not know that I was an Adult Child of an Alcoholic; therefore, I was easy bait to be taken hostage by pathological behavior patterns.

I wanted too much to please her. I tried to adapt in any way I could to keep everything peaceful. If she said to let her sleep instead of going to the afternoon meeting, I let her sleep. When she said I shouldn't bother her with so much detail, I didn't. I was to learn later that this pattern of trying to keep peace at all costs is a symptom of a role picked up in childhood—do or say anything to help prevent Mom from going into a tirade.

This was only perpetuating her problem though, because as long as she could dominate me and keep me operating out of fear of what she would do, she was operating out of a position of control. If she could control me, she surely would never think that she was helpless to handle her drinking problem.

There was no way to please her on this trip. It was a perpetual "catch 22" situation, "damned if I do and damned if I don't." I learned a very valuable lesson there which I want to share with you.

Pride

My younger daughter would often say to me, after we had had a disagreement, "Mom, you are so proud. Why can't you ever apologize? I have never heard you say you were wrong or sorry for anything.''

I didn't know why, but God was refining me, so He set up a situation that caused me to discover the root of that problem of pride.

It couldn't have happened any other way except in a situation where we had to live together for a short time without any other family member intervening. So there we were in a beautiful motel, eating out and having the freedom to choose to go to hear some super teaching, or to go shopping or to visit friends and relatives.

By the third day she was tired and requested that I not bother with so many details, like who was speaking and what time, etc. She also asked me to let her sleep. So I did.

Around 5:00 that afternoon I very quietly fixed my make-up in the bathroom and very carefully changed into my evening meeting clothes. Five minutes before it was time for me to leave, Mom woke up. She asked me why I didn't wake her up in time for her to go with me. Then followed many accusations about how thoughtless I was, and how could I do this to her.

As I sat there listening I realized I had made a mistake by not waking her up. I said, "Mom, I'm sorry. I really made a mistake by not waking you up.''

Insight

The following scene was similar to what one would expect after throwing gas on a fire. She came at me with her fists flying, and I immediately had a flashback to when I was a little girl. I then realized for the first time in my adult life the reason I avoided apologizing. It was programmed into me that *when I opened my mouth to say I'm sorry, the fight would get worse.*

This doesn't make any sense, but when dealing with

alcoholism, one is dealing with craziness. When we were little children, we didn't know that the parent was acting crazy. All we could surmise was that we were the crazy ones.

I kept a little diary that week, October, 1986:

Why Apologizing Is Hard

If you are living with an addict, and are told that you are crazy, or you often feel guilty—I want to tell you, you are not crazy or guilty. Living with an addict is impossible without some relief.

Get relief—Jesus, deliverance or a prayer partner to call on in a crisis.

I know—God let me recently experience this situation and I learned some new insights of why I still had some ungodly reactions to certain stresses. I then realized that in childhood my alcoholic parents kept me in a no-win situation, (damned if you do and damned if you don't).

Without knowledge of spiritual warfare I would not have survived (psychologically) this recent week. But I understood who was my enemy (not Mom, but the demons using her). For relief I went to a friend for prayer, and I shopped by myself.

Remember, I am still not aware that I am an ACoA, and I wrote the following in the arena during the praise and worship services at the Women's Aglow convention in Milwaukee:

Dear God, I want so much for You to like me. I want so much for her to like me. I used to think it was, "I reap what I sow"—therefore I deserve it; but, Lord, could it be that I am not yet dead to self? Did I pick up these patterns because I wanted to be loved and then when I was misunderstood—then what?

Lord, show me. Who am I? Am I an outgoing, friendly person who becomes melancholy from being misunderstood? Or am I a quiet introvert who is trying to please, to gain approval?

Help me, Lord, to be dead to self, so I can be myself and not someone I am not. I was told not to tell her any more, her mind was small—then when I had to let her know I was taking a change of clothes because we weren't returning to our room, she said, 'Why did you wait till now?'

Another confusing comment was, 'Is it too dark for you to sleep?' "

After a few minutes of spending time with the Lord in song and prayer, these words came to me from the Holy Spirit:

"I have plans for you above any you have dreamed. I love you and am preparing you for that time. I will not let you be destroyed. I will heal your relationship with your mom in My time (don't struggle). These trials are preparing you for My service. You have much talent and a way with people that I can use. Laugh like Glenda said."

Helped

It has been said that alcoholics don't have relationships, they take hostages. How true. My encounter with Mom after her nap escalated until she was accusing me of being on drugs, insane and in need of a psychiatrist. Her demons succeeded in making me cry. I decided to abort the trip and fly back home—which seemed to satisfy her. Once the demon was fed by reducing me to tears, Mom returned to acting more "normal." Is that pattern familiar to you? Let me repeat it:

Once the demon reduced me to tears, it was satisfied, and Mom returned to acting more "normal."

I didn't go home, though. On another floor of the hotel some friends who were also at the conference ministered to me and prayed for me, enabling me to laugh again.

A visit with several of my aunts turned out to be very fruitful. At lunch, while Mom was taking one of her "walks" (for a cigarette and drink), I finally got up the courage to ask my aunt some questions that bothered me since I was a small child. I needed to know if my feeling of being an outsider (a member of a family that was also seen as different by someone other than myself) was accurate. I found out that Mom had always been considered "different." She was the eleventh of twelve children, and her tales of their childhood sound like alcoholism affected her family, too.

That helped me not to be so paranoid and guilty about the feelings I had experienced and the observations I had made over the years. You see, as Adult Children of Alcoholics, we end up doubting our own perception of life. We lose our ability to believe that what we see is what is real. As a result of this doubt in self, we don't respond—denial. I needed another respected person to tell me the truth before I could again believe that I was able to make accurate observations. I needed this before I could trust myself to discern what is really going on.

CHAPTER TWELVE

Freedom to Face It

Ignorance makes you a slave to another man's
wisdom [or his demons].   —Anonymous

It was happening. I thought I knew all the answers by
now, yet my life was getting out of control again. Maybe
it was just exhaustion, I reasoned, and a little trip to visit
my children would refresh me. Little did I realize I was
reverting to my old patterns of running and denial.

At this time our home Bible study had grown into an
international ministry called Spiritual Warfare Ministries,
and we were now engaged in training others about the
many aspects of deliverance and spiritual warfare (how
to pray more effectively).

The previous week we had just finished a very successful Spiritual Warfare Training Conference in Lake
Wales, Florida. This was our first, and it was well
attended. The presence and anointing of God rested on
all the guest speakers, and those who attended were

encouraging us to make this an annual affair. (Which we have done.)

The experience of having a conference gave us a fresh empathy for anyone who sponsored a meeting of that magnitude. Our whole staff was exhausted. Now, after months of pressure, I was feeling confused and depressed. I was having difficulty carrying on a conversation with our houseguests (one of the conference speakers and his family). So, with Ken's blessing, I got in my car and headed to another city.

The Trip

God had other plans for me. However, it took several months to see His purpose in the sequence of events that followed. First of all, on the interstate highway, going full speed, my transmission went whirrrrrrr, and soon I realized that the car was just coasting. I pulled over to the shoulder and found that only the low gear would work. For the next forty miles or so, until the next exit, I had to drive at twelve miles per hour.

Have you ever followed someone down the highway that was going super slow? It's awful being the one who is responsible for holding up all the traffic! In my rear view mirror I could see the drivers approaching, then watch the expression on their faces change as they would hit their brakes and swerve to avoid hitting my car in the rear end. In my whole life that was probably the most cursing ever directed toward me.

Finally an exit! But my hopes were quickly dashed— the attendant at the gas station couldn't help me because it was a Sunday, and this exit was in the middle of nowhere. I had to get back on the interstate and double back until it joined a regular four-lane highway which took me back to another exit. I was just two hours away from home at regular speed, but it was impossible to try to get home. The car and I were both in terrible condition by that time. That day I spent six hours on the highway driving twelve miles per hour with the windows rolled down, because the air conditioning didn't work either. For some reason horrible fumes were emitting from the underside of my car making me dizzy.

By the grace of God I made it to a motel. I figured the devil was attacking me as a result of the conference; I wasn't going to give him any more opportunities. I locked myself in my room, too cautious to go to the restaurant for dinner. I called room service instead, and had chocolate cake for supper to drown my sorrows. (A spirit of self-pity can make anyone fat!)

The next day after the repairs were completed, I headed back home. Before I got there I stopped at several car dealerships. My old car was no longer reliable for out of city travel, and I purchased a new car after consulting with Ken.

The next day I repacked my new Mercury and again headed to see my two sons. My younger son was a student at the state university and my other son, my oldest, was there with the automobile executives who were playing in a golf tournament.

By the time I got there the older son had already left with his company to return home. My other boy was busy with class and a job; so there I was, alone in a motel with no more opportunity to stay too busy to face the reality of my past. **My years of running came to a screeching halt!**

Isolation

The next several hours were spent in my room where I cried. I had finally realized that in the new life that I had created since I had been saved and remarried I had avoided developing any friendships. The scar called "Fear of getting hurt again" had so bound me that I had carefully avoided new relationships. I made sure no one got close enough to reject me again. I was totally alone with no one to call except my husband; but he had done all he could. I needed a girlfriend.

When I realized that I was getting nowhere by crying, I dressed and did the next best thing I knew: *I went to the mall*. There I finally bought a book on the subject of Adult Children of Alcoholics. The information in the book hit the "giant of denial" between the eyes and forced me to face the fact that I was an ACoA, and I needed help.

Pride

Two years prior to admitting my need for help, I was at Florence Littauer's C.L.A.S.S. seminar for public speakers. After a personality profile was done, the counselor told me that I had to face the fact that I was still affected by the alcoholism in my family. I would not follow her advice because I was too proud, believing that I already had the answers. After all, I was in the deliverance ministry where we had observed that most problems are of demonic origin and can be cast out in the name of Jesus.

Well, I was right about the problems being demonic in origin, but I was wrong about how to deal with them. In the past I had studied alcoholism; therefore, I thought there was no need to learn any more about being an Adult Child of an Alcoholic. Besides, I had everything in control, didn't I?

So why was I still so miserable two years later sitting alone in a motel room, reading about myself in a book?

As I read the book I no longer felt unique. I discovered that there were a whole bunch of us denying that the root of most of our problems is alcoholism, even if it is a parent's alcoholism and not our own.

The following is a summary of a few things I discovered:

CHARACTERISTICS THAT DESCRIBE ADULT CHILDREN OF ALCOHOLICS

New Hope for Adult Children of Alcoholics

We become isolated and afraid of people and authority figures. Angry people and personal criticism frighten us. We either become alcoholics ourselves or marry them, or both. Failing that, we find another compulsive personality, such as a workaholic, to fulfill our subconscious need for abandonment.

We view life as victims, and we are attracted to weakness in our love, friendships and career relationships.

We have an overdeveloped sense of responsibility, and it is easy for us to be concerned with others rather than ourselves. This helps us to avoid looking too closely at our own faults, and to avoid responsibility for ourselves. Somehow we feel guilty if we stand up for ourselves instead of giving in to others.

We become addicted to excitement in all our affairs, we confuse love with pity, and we tend to rescue others and try to "fix" them.

We have denied feelings from our traumatic childhood and have lost the ability to express our feelings, because they hurt so much. We cannot express even comfortable feelings such as joy or happiness.

We judge ourselves harshly and fear the judgment of others; yet we also criticize and judge others.

We are terrified of abandonment, and will do almost anything to hold onto a relationship rather than experience the painful feeling of abandonment. We developed this from living in an alcoholic environment where no one was emotionally "there" for us.

As alcoholism is a family disease, we took on symptoms early in childhood and carried them into adulthood. Even though we may never take a drink ourselves, we have acquired unhealthy behavior patterns that have given us difficulty, especially in our intimate relationships.

Awareness

Denial had finally lost its control over my life. Now that I knew that I had been looking at life through distorted perception, the restoration of those heretofore hidden areas of my life could begin. I could cast out all the devils I discerned in my life and denial continued to allow others to remain hidden. Whether I called it a problem or a demon, I couldn't have victory over something that I would not admit I had.

What a shock it was to discover that I had to guess at what normal was. I didn't know that I was guessing, but when I saw it in print I couldn't avoid the truth. Probably more of a surprise to me was the discovery that my entire personality profile had been shaped by a role that I was pressured into adopting in a dysfunctional family. So who was the real me? I had been wondering for two years, ever since the personality profile, if I was a compensated introvert. Or could it be that I was actually born with an outgoing personality, but through a series of criticisms, abuse and broken promises, **I adapted my personality in order to be safe and keep peace in the home?**

God's Gentle Hand

Remember, I was just beginning on this new and exciting journey of discovery. God was gently leading me as I finally faced my past. He would continue to place in my path various aids as He has done in the past. As each raw area was exposed and healed, He would then allow another "situation" that opened up the hidden pain and its present effect on my life. I was starting to get excited now that hope was restored.

Just because I was aware that I had unresolved problems didn't mean that I would immediately recognize everything that was abnormal in my life. Most of my lessons were learned through painful experience. God had a purpose for that—pride had to be kept defeated. Those of us who have chosen the role of one in control tend to be proud. Although I was a young Christian, I had become proud of the fact that I understood spiritual warfare. This pride was shielding me from facing my need for help as an Adult Child of an Alcoholic. God apparently had to allow circumstances that were painful and sometimes frightening. Otherwise, if I learned everything through reading (even if the reading was the Bible) I might become even more proud. "Pride goes before destruction, a haughty spirit before a fall" (Proverbs 16:18).

God's next lesson for me came through an experience with burnout.

CHAPTER THIRTEEN

Burnout

Now that I had finally faced the fact that I was an ACoA, God could finally deal with some of the side effects, the roles adapted as a result of growing up in a dysfunctional family. Next on God's "Fix Nancy" list was restoration from the bondage to the lie, "if I am perfect and work harder, maybe they'll love me."

Some friends presented us with a book titled *How to Beat Burnout* by the Minirth-Meier Clinic. My heart rejoiced when I saw the subject of the book, because I knew that Ken had to read it. For the next few days I made sure it just happened to be available where he would have to pick it up and read it. I left it on the coffee table, by his breakfast, on the nightstand and in the bathroom. Have you ever done that?

I couldn't understand why, but he showed no interest in it. I even talked to God about how desperate the situation was because Ken was such a workaholic (notice how I had diagnosed him). Ken needed to read that book so he would stop making so many demands on me. I had become exhausted from trying to keep up with the schedule he planned. Ken had to learn how to slow down, I told myself.

After days of frustration I picked up the book just to see what *Ken* was going to be learning from this book! It didn't take long for me to see that the book was left for me to read, not him.

Recognizing My Problem

Again I had to recognize that I was the one with a problem that needed attention. Right in front of me on the pages was a description of Nancy Curtis. It described much of what I had been experiencing:

Exhaustion, detachment, distance, boredom, cynicism (questions value of friendships and activities), impatience, irritability ("No one can do it like me"), unappreciated, bitter, angry, blame others for me having poor results, withdrawal or tyrannical, demanding and inflexible, threatened, disorientation (trouble remembering), senile, poor concentration, psychosomatic disorders, stress, depression, blaming others for problems with self, suicide.

How often do we, while in denial, project to others what are actually our own faults? As long as I was convinced that the problems were mostly Ken's fault—I thought he was a workaholic—then there was no way for God to do any restoration in my life.

Now I was faced with a painful awareness of my problems and didn't know what to do about them. That is when I prayed. The Lord was faithful again. He led me to an ad for the upcoming North American Congress on the Holy Spirit that was to be in New Orleans. Praise the Lord, Ken wanted to go also.

As the time approached for the trip, I asked God to please speak to me through one or more of the great speakers that would be there. I knew I needed help and really believed that I would receive ministry at that conference. No longer was I pointing the finger at my husband, but I was teachable and willing to face the truth. The pain was too great to endure much longer.

At one of the meetings the speaker was reprimanding us for criticizing a Christian leader that had fallen into sin. As I listened I told God in my self-righteousness that I thought the speaker was very good, but that maybe the next session would have something for me. I was not guilty of that sin, I rationalized; I never had said anything derogatory about that minister. I had taken the Word seriously and would not "touch God's anointed."

Then the Holy Spirit whispered to me, "What about your husband? Haven't you been picking on him and criticizing him for the busy schedule? **He is your leader!**"

Wow! What had I been doing? I was judging the other Christians for *judging* and all the time I was guilty for doing the same. I was not judging a faraway minister. *I had been judging my husband, my leader.*

Repentance

I finally said, "God, I am so sorry for criticizing my husband. Please forgive me for being unforgiving."

After I prayed that prayer a peace filled my heart, and I was able to clearly realize that I had been blind to a basic principle of the Bible that we teach on regularly. That tenet is found in Matthew 18, the principle of unforgiveness, discussed in Part I of this book.

Can you see what had happened to me? I was turned over to the tormentors because I had unforgiveness in my heart; therefore, those demons that cause burnout had a right to afflict me.

But now I had destroyed those rights and was forgiven. What was God going to show me next?

Remember the Past

The group at this meeting was addressed as if we were all Pharisees. We were told that we had lost our compassion for a hurting person or a Christian in trouble because we had forgotten the pit we were in when Jesus found us.

It had been quite a while since I had really thought about what a mess my life was in when Jesus took over. The Holy Spirit began to stir my memory and helped me to realize that if God would reach out and set up circumstances in my life to bring me out of rebellion, then I was to reach out to other confused, lost people with the same mercy.

The speaker was then led by the Lord to have us minister to each other. He instructed everyone to move to the aisles and those of the same sex were to simply hug each other and weep with compassion, using no words. That was the first time in my life that I ever remembered being held by a woman while I wept. God knew my needs, and apparently the needs of thousands of others in attendance. "No temptation has seized you except what is common to man...." (1 Corinthians 10:13).

Release

I walked out of there feeling so cleansed. It felt like years of suppressed crying had finally been let out. When people experience burnout, they classically lose the ability to feel and express their emotions.

Jesus wept before He raised Lazarus from the dead. There was a new hope in my heart because the emotional aspect of my nature was being restored.

Learning to Laugh Again

The next goody God had on my list of healing experiences was a session with a minister known for a "Holy Spirit Laughter" anointing. It happened.

As he ministered, chuckles started to rise up from several places in the Superdome. For a while I felt left out—that is, until I realized that Jesus was the One upon whom I could give my burdens. So I did. I gave Him my newsletter, my computer, my prayer-partner burden and several more heavy responsibilities that were weighing me down. I ceremonially threw these imaginary burdens into the air, symbolic of tossing them away. As I did, I started to feel light, then giddy. Laughter rose from my belly and made it's way through my lips. It almost felt strange, laughing like that.

How amazing that we can go so long in a depressed state and not even know what we have been missing, like my laughing. The laughing continued into the night and added an exciting dimension to our love life.

Commitment

The 1980's will be remembered as a decade of non-commitment. Marriages are coming apart at appalling rates. Christians are floating from church to church, or experience to experience, then staying home.

One principle that carried me and, therefore, our marriage and ministry through this crisis was commitment. I was committed to serve Jesus Christ no matter what. I still am, and never plan to abandon His ship.

This commitment was instrumental in facilitating what happened next. After the conference's evening sessions there was an altar call with four choices: those who had just gotten saved, those who wanted healing, those who wanted the baptism in the Holy Spirit and those wanting deliverance. The different groups went to four different locations in the Superdome.

The deliverance ministry was led by Don Basham whom we had met and highly respected. There was an announcement that Don needed help from ministers who were seasoned in deliverance. Ken said, "Let's go."

I shuddered because this first day at the conference I was not yet restored and had no desire to get involved in ministry—no energy either. But I was committed to serve the Lord, and I trusted Him to take care of me if He wanted me to help that night. So we went with the deliverance crowd.

There were 1,500 persons gathered in the room under the bleachers when Don announced that he needed help. He didn't want anyone he didn't know to get involved in the deliverance. What a great relief! I sat in the front row with Ken, and we allowed ourselves to receive ministry, instead. God protected me that night.

After the prayer time we introduced ourselves to Don. He remembered us and asked if we would help the next three nights. We said yes.

Enthusiasm Renewed

During the days the Lord "fixed" me, and in the evenings we helped other hurting people. The last night in the deliverance room the crowd was around 2,000.

In an overflow area where stragglers gathered, one young woman screamed loudly. The people around her didn't know what to do, so they did the only thing they could think of, they pinned her to the floor. The screaming continued and Don Basham sent one of his workers to see if she was OK. Other than that, he continued with the deliverance, ignoring the distraction the devil was trying to cause.

After the deliverance service Don and his wife were very tired (they had a booth to take care of all day, and ministry every night), so they slipped out to go home. A small group of people tried to contain the screaming woman who had enough strength to toss a grown man away with one arm. It was then that Ken was approached to do something about this situation. As Ken and I drew near the group I could see that it took five or six men to hold her down.

Ken told them to let her go. He bound the demons as he approached, knowing that it would be safe to turn her loose.

"Or again, how can anyone enter a strong man's house and carry off his possessions unless he first ties up the strong man? Then he can rob his house" (Matthew 12:29). The people ministering to her looked up at Ken in disbelief, but obeyed and removed themselves. When she saw that Ken was the one in charge, she went after him, kicking and attempting to hit him.

Because Ken could discern the operation of evil spirits, and because there was no strength in her attack, he spoke authoritatively, "That's not demons, that's you!"

The demons had been bound, and only a frightened young woman was there defending herself in fear. When she heard that truth, she put her hands up to her face and whimpered, "What is happening to me?"

Ken and I led her to a chair and reassured her that Jesus would set her free and we would not hold her down or hurt her. We then ministered to her.

Each evil spirit that left her did something unique. Ordinarily when we minister there are no theatrics. But, because there were about one-hundred fifty people watching this event, God apparently allowed some demonic manifestations to demonstrate His power in a striking way.

When the spirit of fear was told to leave in the name of Jesus, it threw her head back and spoke through her very clearly, but in a different voice, "I don't have to leave her. She likes me." Then the demon spoke in demonic "tongues." After that she exhaled with a shudder, and she was free.

We ordered about eight other evil spirits to go, and each one did the same thing—uttered some stupid remark, complained in demonic tongues and left with a breath, leaving her limp after each departure.

When each demon left, the crowd responded as if a home run had just been hit. They applauded!

The last evil spirit to leave was called Santeria, a type of witchcraft from the Caribbean islands. When she was free, we gave her some instructions and a very happy woman sat there grinning as we walked away.

Reporters!

Standing nearby were two men. One had a camera and the other had a tape recorder with a flat microphone clipped on his shirt. They approached us and asked us why we could cast the demons out of her and the other group couldn't. We explained that they may not have been in unity, or maybe some of them had little experience.

Finally they identified themselves as reporters from *National Geographic*, and they were doing a story, "Born-Again America," for their magazine. They took us to the hotel dining room and continued to ask questions, interviewing us until the dining room closed at 2:00 a.m. Before we parted they arranged for the photographer, Steve McCurry, to come to Lakeland, Florida to take pictures for the article of Spiritual Warfare Ministries in action.

P.J. Vesilind, the senior writer of the magazine, made this statement about what he saw when we were ministering to the young woman:

"I certainly have never seen people in one room be so moved by what must have been the Spirit of God. We were mystified and awed by what we saw; we weren't ready....it...showed the power of God...."

They sent us the proof later: a two-page color spread of me casting a spirit of voodoo out of a woman. The picture covered most of the page, and the text explained what we did and where we were located.

This recognition and respect by representatives of a well known and respected publication was one way God was rewarding us for keeping our commitment to serve Him.

Disappointment

The article, which included most of the major ministries from the United States, had to be canceled just two weeks prior to publication. Because another ministry's scandal received national exposure, P.J. Vesilind said his editor didn't want the magazine to be labeled as an ambulance chaser. We were disappointed, but we will always remember the time we almost made it into a magazine with eleven million circulation.

We still have the pictures and the memories. The photographer has asked us to call him whenever we are out of the country. He would like to fly to meet us for more pictures. So who knows, maybe someday....

CHAPTER FOURTEEN

Grief

The time finally came when Ken and I knew we had to lovingly confront my mother about her alcoholism. We spent days praying and seeking God for the right words to communicate our concern and love for her. (I even had every passage tagged in my Bible that related to this issue.) She listened attentively as we offered (as her Mother's Day gift) to pay for her month-long stay at a local treatment center. Her reaction surprised us.

"Thank you for loving me so much that you are willing to do this for me. Let me think about it for a few days," she said. Then she went home and decided to join Alcoholics Anonymous. She soon sent me a beautiful letter with the classic statement, "My name is _____, and I am an alcoholic."

For the next few years I had a mom again. Our communication was rational and peaceful for the first time that I could remember. But I knew nothing about the damage this "disease" had wrought in my life.

When a loved one is an addict, we stand by helplessly watching him or her, or we make the standard attempts to "help" the addict, which only contribute to his problem if we haven't understood that neither rescue or ridicule will prevent the addict's downfall. We are deceived so often into thinking that he is actually able to think and communicate in a logical, rational manner. But inside the covering your loved one is in some stage of deterioration (which is really demonization). Only the shell of the person is there.

As a new Christian I believed that the love of Jesus would change everyone's life like it did mine—meaning that anyone could quit like I did. I, too, had been in bondage to alcohol until four months after my remarriage. When Ken and I felt that God wanted us to do more than just go to church, we threw out all the booze and that was that. We never had a desire to drink again. Already knowing that God wanted us to get involved in restoring lives, we started by opening up our home for a Friday night Bible study. Our talk with Mom took place about eight months later.

Denial Again

You may already know what's coming, for anyone who has tried to deal with alcoholism eventually discovers that they are on a roller-coaster ride. Hope, then hopes dashed...over and over again...hope for restoration, followed again by discouragement.

That ominous demonic shadow of denial that accompanies alcoholism generation after generation prevented me from dealing with the reality that Mom had started drinking again. I ignored the signals, rationalizing that she must be tired, or her medicine was making her that way.

The craziness showed up again when my brother got remarried (anyone living with alcoholism is living with insanity). I knew that Mom would be very upset if I didn't show up for the wedding, so I flew back for the occasion. For some reason that I still don't understand, she was angry with me. I had made a special effort to spend twenty-four hours in town for the wedding, and I had a cheerful attitude, but it was impossible to please her.

Looking back, I have a suspicion of what ticked her off. It was at the wedding that I first saw her drinking again. She couldn't resist having the champagne. I didn't say a word, but she was defensive, explaining to me that it was all right for her to have a drink on a special occasion.

I knew that alcoholics can never drink again, but was unwilling to face the inevitable and afraid to confront her. Denial had me in it's grip.

The years passed, and I tiptoed all around the problem, until I started to comprehend spiritual warfare. When I began to understand that alcoholism is not really a disease, but demonic in origin, I could more easily forgive Mom for the horrible things she said—it wasn't actually Mom speaking. She really didn't know what she was doing. Jesus said, "Father forgive them, for they do not know what they are doing" (Luke 23:34).

All I did was pray for her and forgive her, not having the courage to confront her again until about four more years had passed.

Because of the denial, I was duped into believing she would just quit again. Then, after a series of circumstances forced me to face the fact that I was an Adult Child of an Alcoholic and was still being affected by it, I started reading books for ACoA's. What an enlightenment!

Turmoil

Encouraged, I started the process of ***withdrawing*** *so she would hurt enough to get help*. However, the demon of alcoholism was much smarter than I was. I was lured over and over into the belief that she was better. She would call and sound like herself and I would believe that the battle was won.

Later I received a late night drunken call that made no sense. Even though I knew it was not my fault that she drank, the words that would come out of Mom's mouth had the power to make me feel guilty and inadequate, just like they did when I was a little girl. I had a lot to learn about these reactions of mine.

Frankly, I was surprised that I could still get hurt. Now I know that was because denial had caused me to still have ungodly reactions (demons in me) that I was unaware of until she (her demons) "pushed my buttons."

Detachment

One time I decided to say good-bye to her in a ceremonial way. That is, I finally realized that she was no longer there. Her personality had "dissolved in the alcohol" (was taken over by demonic activity or, as some say, possessed), verified by a CAT scan which showed that her brain had shrunk, called a "wet head" by experts in alcoholism. (Research shows that each ounce of alcohol kills 10,000 brain cells. Where her brain used to be is just liquid.) I grieved and "buried" her in my mind. I believed that the real "her" would never resurface again. After I did that, her words had no power to inflict pain. A few years of peace followed because the demons using her couldn't "push any buttons" anymore.

Alcoholics always get worse, so the inevitable happened: she was arrested for "running a red light while under the influence'' while she was on the way to our home for the wedding reception of our oldest son. He was the first of her ten grandchildren.

I had told her when she was invited that this reception would be a sober one. I didn't want her to arrive drunk or to keep going out to her car on the driveway to get drinks. "In other words," I said firmly, "I don't want alcohol to ruin this day like so many other special events had been ruined in the past."

When she didn't show up that night, I gave her the benefit of the doubt. Since she was seventy-two years old I rationalized that she may have just forgotten the correct day. So I waited (denial). The next night she didn't come either, and after many phone calls to hospitals, jails in three counties and the highway patrol, I placed her on the missing persons' list. We didn't know what happened to her. She wasn't in any hospitals along the way, and the highway patrol had no record of any accidents with her. The demon of alcoholism succeeded again at creating turmoil.

On Sunday morning at 4:30 a.m. the phone rang. It was from the county jail where they had my mother. The sheriff saw her name on the computer after I had placed her on the missing persons' list.

He said, "Ma'am, you can come now and bail her out."

"Why is my mother in jail?" I asked.

He told me that she had been arrested for running a red light while drunk. Well, I didn't bail her out, because I had finally learned that rescuing a drunk only helps kill him. Amazingly, I didn't feel guilty. The books written for Adult Children of Alcoholics helped me realize that bailing her out was only going to perpetuate her problem. I was determined not to fall into the role of the *enabler* (see Chapter 4). The Bible said what to do long before these "groups" did. In Hosea 2:6-15, God tells us how

141

to pray for the addict, and that we are not to rescue the addict out of His hand. I had been praying a hedge of thorns around her, so I had peace about not rescuing her:

"Therefore I will block her path with thornbushes; I will wall her in so that she cannot find her way. She will chase after her lovers but not catch them; she will look for them but not find them. Then she will say, 'I will go back to my husband as at first, for then I was better off than now.' She has not acknowledged that I was the one who gave her the grain, the new wine and oil, who lavished on her the silver and gold—which they used for Baal. 'Therefore I will take away my grain when it ripens, and my new wine when it is ready. I will take back my wool and my linen, intended to cover her nakedness. So now I will expose her lewdness before the eyes of her lovers; **no one will take her out of my hands**. I will stop all her celebrations: her yearly festivals, her New Moons, her Sabbath days—all her appointed feasts. I will ruin her vines and her fig trees, which she said were her pay from her lovers; I will make them a thicket, and wild animals will devour them. I will punish her for the days she burned incense to the Baals; she decked herself with rings and jewelry, and went after her lovers, but me she forgot,' declares the LORD. 'Therefore I am now going to allure her; I will lead her into the desert and speak tenderly to her. There I will give her back her vineyards, and will make the Valley of Achor a door of hope. There she will sing as in the days of her youth, as in the day she came up out of Egypt' " (Hosea 2:6-15, emphasis added).

Alcoholics need to experience the results of their

behavior or they will never realize they have a problem. If we interfere with God when He is dealing with them, they will never reach that valley where their recovery can begin.

Poor Mom was so frustrated because she couldn't lie to me about where she was that weekend. When she called me, she tried to tell me that she had been in the hospital and that her car was being fixed (it actually was impounded). She didn't have any power over me this time because I had the facts. It's hard to know when an addict is lying, and it certainly was nice to be armed with the truth.

I really believed that this reality of being arrested would bring her face to face with her "problem." But, as the literature and the Bible say, the worse an alcoholic gets, the less they think they have a problem at all:

> "Who has woe? Who has sorrow? Who has strife? Who has complaints? Who has needless bruises? Who has bloodshot eyes? Those who linger over wine, who go to sample bowls of mixed wine. Do not gaze at wine when it is red, when it sparkles in the cup, when it goes down smoothly! In the end it bites like a snake and poisons like a viper. Your eyes will see strange sights and your mind imagine confusing things. You will be like one sleeping on the high seas, lying on top of the rigging. 'They hit me,' you will say, 'but I'm not hurt! They beat me, but I don't feel it! When will I wake up so I can find another drink?' " (Proverbs 23:29-35).

Mom later told me that she didn't call us while she was in jail because she didn't want us to know where she was. She preferred to let us think she was dead.

Enlisting the help of her personal physician, my

brother, experts from the different treatment units, and friends made little difference in the treatment of Mom's alcoholism.

She called me once after that and apologized for all the horrible things she said to me and claimed to be attending AA again. She thanked me for loving her enough to try to get her into the treatment program, but she continued drinking. I am thankful that I have a good memory of her, one conversation in which she expressed her love for me (see anthology at the end of this section). I will treasure that memory.

Mom has wanted to die since I was a little girl, and her choice seems to be slow suicide by alcoholism. No one has been able to stop her; so until God intervenes, she will have to travel this journey alone. I will see to it that she is cared for and comfortable and safe. I will visit her, but she (her demons) can't make me feel bad anymore.

I have learned that **the greatest love I can offer my mother is to refuse to go with her through spiritual and emotional bondage**. Love requires hard choices.

A MINI—ANTHOLOGY
OF FAMILY POETRY

One of my daughters "repeated the patterns" of her parents and began to drink. She couldn't quit and eventually was kicked out of college. After much prayer for her, she eventually made the deans list in nursing school and has received many letters of praise from patients, their families and the staff at the hospital where she now works in intensive care.

As you read this poem, you can see where she was. Let her life be an encouragement for you to keep on praying for your loved ones.

CRUISING—BOOZING

Driving down Cleveland Heights
  With beer on my mind.
Knowing that school
  Was left way behind.
By the feel of my spirits
  I knew Friday was here
So I pulled into Kau-Kau
  And bought my first beer.
Cruising the streets
  With a beer in my hand
My passengers knew
  That I was in command.
Two sixes were gone
  Driving became hard.
When I came to
  I was parked in my yard.
I staggered into my house
  With beer on my breath
And when I saw my parents
  I knew it was my death.
I learned my lesson
  And still go cruising
But never again
  Will I go boozing.

Those of us who have grown up with the unpredictable emotional swings of the addict often wonder who we are. Our identity, especially when young, is dependent on what we see reflected from those who are supposed to love us.

I will never really understand Mom's motive for writing this, because her opinion of my life was a constant variable between how wonderful I was and how awful I was. Often the "wonderful" statements were a "set up" that left me completely disarmed for an attack.

Nevertheless something within me treasures this gift from my mother's heart. It was written about the same time my daughter wrote the previous poem. My Dad had died five years earlier.

A TOAST TO NANCY

(An Image of Faith, Courage and Integrity)

How very proud we are of you—
We've always been; you know that's true.
You've braved your hurts, you still can smile
You've helped us see, your life's worthwhile.

You've suffered much, yet bore your grief
In such a way, one has belief
In God's great love, His saving grace.
If we but pray, all cares erase.

Throughout your years of smiles and tears
You've come this far in forty years
To show the world what you're made of.
For that I thank the Lord above
For all you've done—will always do
To pave the way, to see the "blue"
Thru problems that may lie ahead
Your faith and courage will help instead
Of doubting, fearing and wondering "WHY"
So many things can go awry.

You'll "hang-in-there", you'll see it thru
'Cause best of all, dreams do come true.

Oh! How I wish that Dad were here"
To share this joy, to toast our cheer
Yet, we all know that surely he
Is with us now...
...shares heartfelt glee.

So here's to you, our daughter dear!
God be with you throughout this year!

My daughter (the one who I left crying on the driveway so I could smoke) wrote the following poem after God came to her rescue through Youth With a Mission. She wrote it at age sixteen while on the road ministering with YWAM.

She had suffered terrible insecurity because I was incapable of being a good mom. My own "scars" and "confusion" had me bound. But God was faithful to bring healing and give her a direction for her life, as this poem illustrates.

THE PATH

There was a straight and narrow path
  Between my dusty feet,
Until I turned my head and saw a trail
  That all my wants it seemed to meet.

This new trail seemed to be so wide
  With many ways to go
This downhill walk was easier
  The pace was not so slow.

As I continued down this trail
  Aware I soon became,
That this trail led to my destiny;
  My life is not a game.

Broken people were everywhere
  Just bumping into walls
With blinded eyes and deafened ears
  In desperation calls.

Now I feel this trail is not the way
  This place is not for me,
The correct path was the other one
  Praise God I now can see.

I quickly turned and walked uphill
  Back **up** to my first ole trail,
So tired did my legs become
  I felt I was to fail.

Then suddenly I heard a voice
  And felt a hand in mine
With strength that picked me from the ground
  And helped me start my climb.

O Praise the Lord I see "THE WAY"
  He's right before my face
He's telling me "I'm on your side,
  You'll finish soon this race."

This is a strait and narrow path
  Beneath my dusty feet
There is One Friend so close to me
  Who all my **needs** will meet.

PART III

Praying and Healing:
The Deliverance Phase

CHAPTER FIFTEEN

Victory Over Old Reactions

There have been two avenues that I have followed in response to illness or injuries: the **before Christ** reaction, and the **after Christ** response. As I've stated already, most of my life patterns were the same after I was saved, including the methods the devil used to attack me. My reaction to these attacks is what changed. Now I could reach God through prayer and expect miracles. Because of this, the outcome of the attacks has been different.

The first time I broke my ankle was while playing tennis with the local tennis team. It happened before I was a Christian while I was still taking courses in preparation for nursing school. I was still married to my first husband, locked into a role as a victim. I responded in a predictable manner to the situation. "Poor me. I've tried so hard, and now look at what's happened."

It was my right ankle which was broken, so driving a car was a challenge. The day of the injury was also an exam day. While my cast was still wet, my sister-in-law drove me to school and waited for me to finish my exams.

The next several months were trying, because I had the accident when life was beginning to become a challenge. These challenges should have been exciting, but for me they were scary. At this time in my life a friend from my Transactional Analysis training group and I were setting up a seminar at our local church. The ads were out and we were prepared to teach people the wonders of humanism. (Remember, this was before Christ.) During this season in my life I had taken up jogging and was beginning to get physically fit.

Avoidance Maneuver

It's important to note here that the fitness and the seminar both had the potential of leading me into unknown territory. The exercise could make me more attractive and the seminar would force me out of hiding and put me in the public eye. An ACoA still in denial (like I was) needs predictability in order to maintain control. Since the territory ahead was unpredictable, I subconsciously resorted to one of my patterns of escape—an accident.

Ken and I have since learned that the tendency to have accidents is a result of demonic activity let in by reacting in a sinful way. For example, resentment toward those who have abused or neglected us in the past opens the door to tormenting spirits (Matthew 18).

The seminar was cancelled, and I quit jogging; but I didn't quit school. I drove the car with my left foot instead of my right. That way I could feel like someone special—a poor accident victim finding a way to continue schooling.

When the cast was taken off I could be a heroine again. With much pain, discoloration and swelling, I returned to walking and jogging. I liked being seen as a brave person, enduring all that discomfort to get back into shape. The truth was, I was relieved that I didn't have to teach a seminar. I wouldn't admit that I was too frightened to keep my commitment.

New Territory—After Christ

The second time I broke the same ankle the circumstances were quite different. It was just over a year later. During that year I was in nursing school, entered several races, including a marathon (I have my fourth place medal on the shelf along with my children's many trophies), and was going through a divorce. (How's that for new territory?) But this time I was a Christian. The same demonic pattern from childhood caused the "accident," but the course after this injury was quite different.

I fell as I was passing the number eighteen tee on the golf course, four miles into my five mile run that drippy morning. All I could think of was, "Why now, God?" The snapping sound of the bone breaking as my foot turned over was familiar now. After sitting in the mud for a few minutes, crying and wondering how I was going to get help, I realized that I wasn't. No one was going to be going past this area for at least another half-hour (it was 7:30 a.m.). It was too cold that February morning to sit there and wait, so I decided to tough it out and walk home. ACoA's have been well trained to endure pain.

At the house I was greeted by my sixteen-year-old son who was so alarmed at the size of the swelling that he drove me to the emergency room. There he saw the x-rays with me. The break had separated the edges of the bone by one quarter of an inch. Because there was so much swelling the doctor wrapped my ankle in an ace bandage and told me to go home and keep it elevated for thirty-six hours. Then I could return for the cast.

He said, "I will write a note letting your instructor know that you can't take care of any patients for several weeks." He gave me a pain-pill prescription, and my son took me home.

Depressed, I went to bed with my medicine, not understanding why I would have to get hurt when my life was just becoming exciting and manageable. (This was just three months into my new life with the Lord.) The pain was so bad that when one of the children came to visit me and sat on the edge of the bed, the jagged edges of bone would rub and tears would roll down my cheeks.

That night, my new boyfriend (who is now my husband) came to see me. We had known each other just a few weeks. He was a new Christian, too, and that night we were supposed to go to a covered dish dinner at his pastor's home.

He told me, "God will heal your ankle."

My response was, "I don't think so. Maybe God wants me to be laid up for a while to teach me a lesson."

"I believe that He will heal you, Nancy. When I go to the dinner tonight, I'll ask them all to pray for you, and I believe that God will heal your ankle," Ken responded.

This was all new to me, and I exhibited great lack of faith, but Ken just kept encouraging me. By the time he left I was actually hoping that God would heal my ankle.

That night I went to sleep wondering whether I should anticipate a miracle, risking disappointment if it didn't happen, or believe that nothing would happen so I wouldn't be "let down." Despite my doubt, God was about to turn my life around, so I would never again react to calamity as in the past.

My First Miracle!

With the morning came a strange peace. I was awake for a few minutes before realizing that I had not taken any pain medicine since 11:00 p.m. the night before. The next thing noticeable was the lack of pain in my foot. Excitement surged through me as I carefully lowered my bandaged leg off the bed. Slowly I pressed my foot to the floor. **No pain!**

"WOW!" I shouted. Unwrapping the ankle I walked to the shower without crutches. God had healed me just like Ken had said He would.

My son was shocked when he saw me. This was his first experience with a real healing miracle, and for him it was so real because he had seen the original injury and the x-ray.

That day I showed up in the hospital's orthopedic ward for my nursing class walking normally. My instructor turned as white as her uniform and muttered, "I know God does miracles, but I have never seen Him fix bones before."

My First Christian Race

When I was a young Christian and was rejoicing over a miracle, usually I would tell my pastor's wife about it in the hallway at church. She encouraged me to write my testimonies down for their church magazine. The following is one I shared on Joyce Strader's show, "Heart to Heart," on WCIE, 91.1 FM.

The following is the original as I first wrote it several years ago. It reflects some of the new responses I had learned in thwarting attacks that formerly had the power to defeat me.

Ken, my husband, drove me to the Lake Mirror Civic Center one hour before race time. While we waited, I shared with him my strategy for the race. Four years ago I ran so slow that they didn't even keep the streets closed for me. This time I felt I was in good form for the event. There was an air of pride in my voice as I stated how I would hold my speed in check at the beginning, and gradually increase my speed for the last three miles.

The day was hot and sunny. The starting time was 8:30 a.m. and we were to run on the streets around three lakes. My shoes were new, and ordinarily I run on grass in the early morning when it's cooler.

The race was dedicated to the glory of God, and I was feeling confident as I approached the starting line. A JOGGING FOR JESUS logo was on my shirt, and I really felt the presence of the Holy Spirit that morning.

The race started, and so did the harassment from the enemy. Less than one-third way around Lake Mirror "it" happened. A little old lady with curly white hair and skinny legs passed me! That provided Satan with his first opening—pride. I started getting thoughts like —"You can't let a 60 year old woman pass you up like that, you must have started too slow, why don't you try to pass her up?"

So I started running faster. And I couldn't catch up with her! At the first mile the timer called out 10 minutes and 36 seconds and I know then that I had been running too fast. But I was still allowing myself to be prodded by pride and continued to try to catch up with my "adversary."

At the two-mile mark my pace was still too fast, and I was in trouble. A quick check showed my pulse to be near 180 beats per minute. (I often run it up that far, but with four miles to go that was too high.) So again the devil fired— "Now you've done it. You won't be able to finish this race. See what you did? You blew it trying to run so fast."

I started to think (finally)! "If Jesus can help and heal others, then He will heal me of this problem if I ask Him." So first I came to the Lord in prayer and confessed my sins of pride, etc., at the beginning of the race. Then I told Satan to get off my case. After that I promised to give God all the glory, and would He please slow down my pulse so I could finish the race?

Praise the Lord that Jesus made this all possible! He touched me and returned my heartbeat to a safe rate.

The next two miles were hot and uneventful. Lake Hollingsworth was beautiful, and I enjoyed watching the scenery and praying. A wet sponge was handed to me. I saw another runner squeeze it over the back of his neck, so I did the same. It was refreshing, but apparently wasn't enough. The signs of heatstroke were upon me. My body stopped sweating and my face was dry.

The "accuser" tried again— "It's too hot for you, your head is going to hurt all day, you can only run when it's cooler, you're too old for this, don't be so foolish."

I said, "In the name of Jesus Christ, Go! I won't listen to you." Then I called on my Lord Jesus again to heal me. I simply asked Him to make my body sweat again so I could finish the race and glorify His name.

Immediately sweat started running down my face and body.

That was the second miracle! I just praised the Lord and kept running.

I knew that I had trained and run this race for a purpose; and although I wasn't sure what that purpose was yet, I was quickly catching on!

Before the five-mile mark my legs suddenly felt peculiar. The fronts of my shins had zipping up and down them sharp pains like electric shocks. The devil quickly jumped on this circumstance and reminded me—"You're not running on grass and you have new shoes on, and besides you're too old, so why don't you just quit now and walk in down those back streets, no one will ever know you didn't finish."

By this time my faith was soaring and I told Satan he was a liar and couldn't tempt me to quit because Jesus would heal me!

Then I asked for the third miracle! "Lord, I know You have come to my rescue twice already today. Please heal my shins so I can finish this race for Your glory."

(At this point the pain disappeared suddenly and completely and never has returned.) P.T.L.

Running became a joy! I was able to start passing other runners. I grinned at the policeman who was at each corner (the same one moved along with us slow runners and kept the cars from hitting us). By the time I was within sight of Lake Mirror, I was singing fairly loudly, "They that wait upon the Lord, shall renew their strength. They shall mount up on wings as eagles.

They shall run and not be weary, they shall walk and not faint. Teach me Lord, teach me Lord, to wait!"

I was able to sprint the last quarter mile to the finish line effortlessly. WOW! The 40-50 age group had six women entered and I finished 6th, but that wasn't what the race was all about.

P.S. Victory is only a prayer away! Jesus is alive! Pain, doubt, fear, infirmities or defeating "attitudes" can be overcome by the Blood of the Lamb! By His stripes we were healed! Praise the Lord! He is so merciful, loving, forgiving, and so close when we reach out to Him.

Our journey through life will also take us to the finish line, and to eternity with Jesus, if we learn to recognize our enemy, avoid what he tempts us with, and each day *turn our whole self and life over to be used by our Lord Jesus Christ. He knows what all our needs are and will guide and direct us to the Father.*

When we keep our eyes on Jesus we will be kept safe and protected from the enemy.

More Than Survival

Remember, I wrote this when I was still a baby Christian. The reason I am sharing that fact with you is so you won't be tempted to avoid confronting the devil because you feel like a novice. No matter what stage of Christian maturity you are, God will hear and answer your prayers. Don't accept old patterns of failure.

Just because something has always been that way doesn't mean that it always will be that way! If I could finish that race, you can finish yours.

Look at the following promises God has for us.

"He who dwells in the shelter of the Most High will rest in the shadow of the Almighty. I will say of the LORD, 'He is my refuge and my fortress, my God, in whom I trust.' Surely he will save you from the fowler's snare and from the deadly pestilence. He will cover you with his feathers, and under his wings you will find refuge; his faithfulness will be your shield and rampart. You will not fear the terror of night, nor the arrow that flies by day, nor the pestilence that stalks in the darkness, nor the plague that destroys at midday. A thousand may fall at your side, ten thousand at your right hand, but it will not come near you. You will only observe with your eyes and see the punishment of the wicked. If you make the Most High your dwelling—even the LORD, who is my refuge—then no harm will befall you, no disaster will come near your tent. For he will command his angels concerning you to guard you in all your ways; they will lift you up in their hands, so that you will not strike your foot against a stone. You will tread upon the lion and the cobra; you will trample the great lion and the serpent. 'Because he loves me,' says the LORD, 'I will rescue him; I will protect him, for he acknowledges my name. He will call upon me, and I will answer him; I will be with him in trouble, I will deliver him and honor him. With long life will I satisfy him and show him my salvation' " (Psalm 91).

You see the key to living a life far above mere survival is found in the first two verses of this psalm. That is what I was doing in the race—dwelling in the secret place of the Most High; therefore, I was able to enjoy a victory far greater than winning first place.

Patterns Then and Now

I spent so much of my life as an invalid before I

understood the source of my problems. When I was in my early thirties I dieted for a year and lost fifty pounds. Several things happened as a result of the weight loss:

(1) My husband came to the Weight Watcher's meeting and witnessed the ceremony where I received a diamond pin, but he never recognized that I had lost any weight—rejection.

(2) My metabolism got messed up because I had omitted all grains from my diet for that period of time.

(3) I started having problems with my heart. It would pause and then beat rapidly—over 200 beats per minute.

The ACoA pattern that I was unaware of was again presenting itself. This time the new and scary territory was a slim body. Men were telling me how good I looked. I didn't feel safe. The rest of that year was spent undergoing tests to find the cause of the paroxysmal tachycardia and gaining back the weight I had lost. I acted like an invalid, afraid I would have a tachycardia attack if I ventured far from home. After that year had passed I didn't have any cardiac irregularities for about fifteen years.

Recently it was discovered that I have a prolapsed mitral valve. This was the probable cause of my early distress and has been implicated as the cause of some more recent alarming problems.

Christian Authority

The difference is in how I react to the problem. Now that I know that I have authority over all demonic power, and that illness and disease are caused by the devil, my response to colds, flu, pain, or heart irregularities is quite different than before. Now I understand spiritual warfare.

Several years ago, for example, we were preparing to have a *Spiritual Warfare Training Conference* in Oakland, California. Because of the amount of satanic attack aimed at us and the ministry, I felt that God wanted me to go to the mountains in North Carolina to fast and pray for the conference. On the way I went to visit my son in Tallahassee and daughter and another son in Atlanta. The morning I was to leave Atlanta for the mountains I awoke with a sore throat, severe sinus pain and dizziness.

My thoughts were drifting between should I stay at my daughter's home and let her nurse me through this? or, should I try to drive back home and forget the mountains?

Then I wondered if I should treat this as if it was a demonic attack and go to the mountains to fast and pray anyway.

I knew God wanted me to pray for the conference, but I was feeling too sick to walk straight, much less drive four hours into the mountains where I would be all alone.

Defeating Old ACoA Patterns

When in doubt, cast it out. That's what I did.

I said, "You foul spirit of infirmity, I bind you in the name of Jesus. You leave me now. I plead the blood of Jesus (demons can't stand the blood of Jesus) over myself and break any curse coming against me or the conference in the name of Jesus."

Before that prayer, even my tears were burning the skin around my eyes. After I rebuked those spirits I pointed my car toward North Carolina in faith, and before I had reached the Georgia border, God had totally healed me. All the symptoms were gone and I felt alert and energetic without taking a drop of medicine.

Certain patterns in our lives can be traced to demonic

attack or activity, not germs, and not coincidences. We can be a lot more optimistic about our future knowing the cause of our setbacks, because Jesus Christ gave all Christians authority over all demonic power.

The Appalachian Trail

Each day while in the mountains I went walking. Since I got saved as a runner, my best prayer time still continues to be while jogging or walking. I wasn't sure how much endurance I had while fasting, but I wanted to hike up the Appalachian trail one day. That's when I discovered Satan wasn't through with his attacks.

In my pocket was a little *Jesus Pocket Promise Book* that I had forgotten to give to my son in Atlanta. At first I moaned about being so forgetful and was angry at myself for not being organized enough to have given it to him. Soon I would discover God's plan for that book.

I also had my video camera along because the scenery was so breathtaking that October day. The path I was taking was above a gate that I had a key for. No one was around, and I had the trail all to myself. Then the path started going down instead of up, and I soon realized that if I continued I could get lost, because I was supposed to be climbing to the top of Big Bald Mountain. I turned around.

Suddenly, without warning, my heart began to beat very irregularly. My chest hurt, and I was getting dizzy. I had two choices: one was to try to walk back up the hill to the main road and down to my car; the other was to sit down on a rock that was there and rest until I recovered. But there were thousands of bumble bees swarming among the flowers all around the rock.

I could hear the devil saying, "If you sit on this rock the bees will sting you, and if you try to walk uphill in this condition you will have a heart attack, because you are in a high altitude and have been fasting. Besides that, no one will be walking through this remote place for days. So it's a hopeless situation.''

The Devil Is a Liar

There was no way that I could walk, so I sat on the rock and rebuked the bees. I also realized that I was dealing with a spirit of fear again, and I felt that I needed another scripture to battle that demon, so I asked God to show me one. I soon discovered why I still had the little *Jesus Pocket Promise Book.* While sitting on the rock I read page after page of Bible promises.

My heart was still pounding wildly and I was harassed with thoughts like, No one will pass here for days, and no one knows where you are.

On this trip I had been doing a scripture study about not being in bondage to our past. I sat there confidently reading God's Word, believing that He would restore me and I wouldn't have to be an invalid or have to be rescued as in the past.

Then Isaiah 41:10 leaped out at me: "So do not fear, for I am with you; do not be dismayed, for I am your God. I will strengthen you and help you; I will uphold you with my righteous right hand.''

God told me to sit there on that rock and memorize that verse and He would heal me. I did and He did. I took videos as I confidently walked out of the woods repeating, So do not fear....

The devil is always defeated by the name of Jesus, the Blood of Jesus, or the Word of God.

Commitment vs. Escape

Before Christ any kind of infection always seemed to

turn into a major castastrophe—like the time I got mastitis.

I breast-fed my first baby until he had hernia surgery at six weeks of age. A severe case of mastitis ended that experience, and my doctor said that I could never nurse a baby again.

When we moved, I didn't let my new obstetrician know about the history of mastitis. With great satisfaction I nursed my other babies.

When the fifth baby was born, I knew he would be the last one, and this was the end of a phase of my life that was so fulfilling. At the same time I was trying to live a social life that left me exhausted most of the time. In the flurry of demands that I could not keep up with, "it" happened again.

The baby was less than two months old. I was getting ready for a bridge and dinner party when I noticed, along with the pain in my breast, that I was feeling very chilly. In less than one hour my temperature rose to over 104 degrees. I got out of hostessing the party, but had to sacrifice my last few months of breast-feeding.

Depression set in because I was deprived of something I loved to do. I treasured those intimate times with my fifth baby. I had no idea why the pattern of getting sick under pressure plagued my life like a curse.

Winning This One

Years later, after Spiritual Warfare Ministries was established, we were invited to minister in the Bahamas. The week-long revival was to take place in Sandy Point on the south tip of Abaco, Bahamas. That spring the flu epidemic was claiming victims all around the country. It looked like I was one of them.

The fever and symptoms hit me a week before we were

to leave for Sandy Point. I got so weak that all I could manage was getting to the bathroom. Meanwhile, we were all aware that there was much voodoo where we were going, and suspected that my illness might be a result of a curse. Instead of giving in to it, like I had with the mastitis, Ken and several others with the ministry prayed for me all week. It still looked like I wouldn't be able to go. My doctor didn't want to prescribe antibiotics, and I was too sick to cook, eat or pack. Ken arranged to take another man with him and leave me home.

The morning the plane was to leave, even though I was still feeling weak and puny, I got out of bed, took a shower, packed and climbed into the car. I was believing that I was healed. We flew out of Fort Lauderdale and by the time the plane landed I felt great! That same night we did our first church service in Sandy Point and for six more days and nights continued to minister on the streets, in homes and in the church. I was so strong and full of energy it was as if I had never been sick at all. It was the devil that made me sick, but as the result of intercessory prayer, the curse was overcome.

Saint Paul wrote to the Corinthians after he almost was overcome:

"We do not want you to be uninformed, brothers, about the hardships we suffered in the province of Asia. We were under great pressure, far beyond our ability to endure, so that we despaired even of life. Indeed, in our hearts we felt the sentence of death. But this happened that we might not rely on ourselves but on God, who raises the dead. He has delivered us from such a deadly peril, and he will deliver us. On him we have set our hope that he will continue to deliver us, **as you help us by your prayers**" (2 Corinthians 1:8-11, emphasis added).

Dealing With Mom

In the old days every holiday, birthday or other special occasion was spoiled because Mom would get so nasty when she drank.

Before I understood the authority I had over her demons, I just dreaded these family gatherings. On almost all of those special occasions, Mom would get so mean that the children would quietly slip out and I would end up in tears.

Then we discovered that we could pray over our house and bind the demonic activity so that it could not manifest because of the power of God. Several things happened then. Either she couldn't stand to stay and left to go home early with some excuse, or she would stay, but was unable to get mean.

Cursed

Three years ago my daughter reminded me of a statement I had made when they were all little. I had quoted a statistic that I had heard on television which said, "Out of every five live births only four live to become adults." My daughter said that because of my statement they all wondered, as they grew up, which one of them was going to die.

One son was affected more by that curse than the others. He was the accident-prone one. This son fell off the high-dive, knocked out his front teeth, tore his knee open biking and had two serious car accidents. Finally he called from college and said that the doctor had diagnosed a malignant melanoma which was to be removed by a surgeon. The doctor had already called my son's dad and told him of the seriousness of the situation. Our boy had let it grow too long.

Then my son told me that he always knew he was

171

going to die before he grew up. I asked him if he would like me to lead him through a prayer so God could heal him. He agreed. We prayed, and the next week the report came back from the pathologist—he no longer had a melanoma, but a simple basal cell carcinoma which was totally removed.

"God changed the mole after we prayed," my son told me.

No Longer a Victim

Before I made Jesus Christ Lord of my life, getting sick or hurt meant that "poor me" was a victim again.

After Christ, a setback of illness or injury (with very few exceptions when God is trying to correct patho-logical patterns in my behavior or attitudes that are destructive to me) meant that the devil was trying to keep me from accomplishing something. Since I can do all things through Christ Who strengthens me, I no longer dread an unpredictable future. I no longer have to get sick or hurt to escape a responsibility. If God wants me to do it, He then makes a way for me to do it. He has given me the equipment to deal with the devil when the attacks come. In fact, God has made a way for all of us to have victory.

A complete teaching of how to pray over your home, business or property is in our first book, *Tormented*. You will need that information. We have received hundreds of letters joyfully sharing the wonderful changes in homes and businesses as a result of learning how to fight the devil.

We'll share with you some of the basics of spiritual warfare in the last section of this book, so you won't have to go through life like a cork in a stream.

CHAPTER SIXTEEN

Deliverance From Fear

Before our first wedding anniversary, a miracle more life changing for me than the healed ankle took place. This miracle stripped off the first layer of my ACoA mask.

We overcome the devil with the blood of the Lamb and the word of our testimony, according to Revelation 12:11. So the testimonies are for a purpose: to expose and defeat the devil's plans for your life.

There was a time when I couldn't write a thank-you note. When thank you's were in order, I would put off writing so long that eventually, I thought, the gift giver forgot all about the fact that I never acknowledged the gift. Why did I procrastinate like that?

Fear. If I wrote to anyone, then they would read what I wrote. When they read it they might not like the way I expressed myself. Rather than take a chance on being criticized or judged for what I wrote, I simply didn't write. I had a pathological dread of incurring anyone's disapproval. Some may say I was too sensitive, but at the bottom of it all the real cause of my procrastination was fear.

Buried Talents

Another area in which fear had its grips was related to the painting talent God had given me. Would you believe that I could not tolerate the thought of having anyone look at a picture I painted? Of course people did see my paintings, but I couldn't stand it.

I know that children often dread music lessons. But, as the other students were waiting for their turn with the music teacher, they usually were visiting among themselves. I just sat there, paralyzed and sweating, even though I had practiced all week. Actually I was a good musician, but never realized my potential as one because I didn't want anyone to hear me, fearfully dreading their rejection.

Escape Routes

I remember being chosen to be the only trombonist to be part of a small group of eight musicians from the Lakeland Symphony Orchestra to accompany a tympanist playing a Darius Milhaud solo. I knew my part well and could play the difficult passages smoothly, but on the day of the concert I got a migraine headache. Up until the time to play I was laying down offstage in the wings. I couldn't get out of playing because no one else knew the part. I know I did poorly when I did play that night because I had tried to cure the headache with martinis.

As already noted, when the pressures of life became intolerable, or when I couldn't get out of a challenging situation, I got sick, or I had an accident. That was the way I avoided responsibility. These avoidance maneuvers, rooted in fear, persisted throughout most of my adulthood. The world would say that the cause was *subconscious*. The Bible says the cause is *demonic*. "For God did not give us a spirit of timidity, but a spirit of power, of love and of self-discipline" (2 Timothy 1:7).

Adrenalin

Our bodies were equipped by our Creator with a system designed specifically for handling stress. God placed on top of our kidneys a pair of adrenal glands. They are there to provide us with a hormone necessary for the production of the energy needed to beat up an attacking bear or run away from it. What happens when adrenalin surges through our bodies, and there is no bear to fight or run away from? We get sick. What caused the adrenalin to be pumped through our bodies? Fear. When a bear comes after you, normally you would feel frightened. Then the adrenalin begins pumping, and you find yourself suddenly able to run faster than you ever did in your life. Or you will immediately have the strength to beat up the bear. After the escape or the battle, with the hormone exhausted, you would then feel peace and euphoria because you are safe. This is called the "Fight or Flight Syndrome."

When you dreaded rebuke, rejection or going to work; or if you spent much of your life in fear, wondering "which daddy would be coming home tonight," the adrenalin that was produced during that stressful time wasn't used because you couldn't run away or fight back. (Later in life some of you finally did run or fight.) Since the adrenalin could not be used, it eventually caused high blood pressure, ulcers, headaches or a myriad of other diseases instead.

So can you imagine how excited I felt when, as a young

Christian, I learned that fear is a spirit, and it can be told to leave in the name of Jesus?

Even though there was finally hope for me, I was too timid to get out of my pew to go to the front of the church to receive prayer for fear. For three weeks I sat in misery in church knowing that I could be delivered from a spirit of fear. At the same time I was so bound with fear that I was unable to go up front to be set free from it.

The Miracle

Then I attended a youth service. There I sat while this scripture story was explained:

> "Again, it (the kingdom of God) will be like a man going on a journey, who called his servants and entrusted his property to them. To one he gave five talents of money, to another two talents, and to another one talent, each according to his ability. Then he went on his journey. The man who had received the five talents went at once and put his money to work and gained five more. So also, the one with the two talents gained two more. But the man who had received the one talent went off, dug a hole in the ground and hid his master's money.
>
> "After a long time the master of those servants returned and settled accounts with them. The man who had received the five talents brought the other five. 'Master,' he said, 'you entrusted me with five talents. See, I have gained five more.'
>
> "His master replied, 'Well done, good and faithful servant! You have been faithful with a few things; I will put you in charge of many things. Come and share your master's happiness!'

"The man with the two talents also came. 'Master,' he said, 'you entrusted me with two talents; see, I have gained two more.'

"His master replied, 'Well done, good and faithful servant! You have been faithful with a few things; I will put you in charge of many things. Come and share your master's happiness!'

"Then the man who had received the one talent came. 'Master,' he said, 'I knew that you are a hard man, harvesting where you have not sown and gathering where you have not scattered seed. So I was afraid and went out and hid your talent in the ground. See, here is what belongs to you.'

"His master replied, 'You wicked, lazy servant! So you knew that I harvest where I have not sown and gather where I have not scattered seed? Well then, you should have put my money on deposit with the bankers, so that when I returned I would have received it back with interest.

" 'Take the talent from him and give it to the one who has the ten talents. For everyone who has will be given more, and he will have an abundance. Whoever does not have, even what he has will be taken from him. And throw that worthless servant outside, into the darkness, where there will be weeping and gnashing of teeth' " (Matthew 25:14-30).

This was the youth pastor teaching the kids. I sat there feeling miserable because I knew that God had given me several talents that I was not using. I finally felt so guilty for burying what God had given me that I jumped out of my seat and was the tallest person at the altar call that night. I walked right up to Pastor Karl Strader and told him the I wanted to be delivered from a spirit of fear.

He stood in front of me and very firmly spoke to the demon in me, not to me. He said, "You foul spirit of fear, come out of her in Jesus name." He then told me to breath it out. As I exhaled it felt like several lumps of air left me. After that I felt almost giddy with relief.

After Jesus set me free, I could write *more* than thank-you notes; I am now writing books!

One of the most profound and exciting aspects of the ministry of deliverance is that a problem that had severely hampered me for all of my life simply left me in one moment through a breath. Before that night I was still afraid of telephones, still driven by thoughts like, what will people think, still unwilling to write anything to anyone. After that night I started to look for opportunities to boldly proclaim what God had done for me.

At last, I was free to answer God's call on my life.

CHAPTER SEVENTEEN

Surrender

From the time I was nine years old I knew that God wanted me serve Him. At the time I thought that meant being a missionary. As a young girl the only place I ever felt safe and at peace was in church. I was a very devout Catholic, going to mass and communion every day, not only in grade school where it was mandatory, in high school as well. When I was out of school I walked over a mile to church every morning before walking to work. Even when I was nursing my fourth baby, I would try to get to church across town as much as possible.

The children remember how I used to bring home doughnuts on the days I went to mass. They were very enthusiastic about my "spirituality."

When I was a young Catholic girl, I thought serving God as a missionary meant being a nun and never having a family. So I walked away from God's call on my life. But all through my adult life, whenever I was attending a convention, I would wander around looking for a

179

missions booth to see if there were any opportunities to help in the Lord's work even though I was married and had five children.

Surrender

After my moral decline I didn't think that God would want me any more. But by the time I turned forty God had given me a new life, a new husband, new church and new opportunities as a registered nurse. A major turning point of my life took place a few months after I had taken a course in Old Testament Studies. I discovered that the Bible fascinated me.

On one particular Sunday, as Ken and I were driving to the evening church service, I told him about my childhood desire to be a missionary. Then I proceeded to say, "Well it's too bad that I am so old and female, because if I were younger and a man, I would go to Bible school and become a minister. I enjoy so much seeing miracles happen and watching God restore lives. I sure would like to be able to minister to people, too. Too bad that I'm too old, and that I'm a woman."

That night, after his sermon, Pastor Strader announced that there were fourteen people in the church who had "a call of God on their lives" for full-time ministry. I stood there gripping Ken's hand, looking around the church to see who they would be.

A few went forward.

Then the pastor said that God was tugging on the hearts of several who had resisted His call in the past. It's funny—my heart was really pounding, and I could feel the tug, but I was sure that I was not included in this plea. But when the pastor said there were five more and that God was looking for *older people and women*. That did it! I had been holding on to Ken's hand for dear life, but I knew then that my nursing career was over for now. I was going to be obedient and follow what God had asked me to do thirty-three years earlier. I headed to the altar.

What peace! As soon as I reached the front of the church, thereby making an open commitment to serve God, the peace that surrounded and filled me was incredible. I knew what I had to do and felt no qualms about it.

Prophecy for the Ministry

The next week, while attending Rev. Fran Harrison's Tuesday morning "Campmeeting" at our Assembly of God Church, I went up to the altar area for prayer for healing.

When she walked up to me she didn't pray. Instead she allowed God to use her to speak to me about the ministry in which He was going to use us. To the best of my memory it went something like this:

> "My child, you have been obedient. You have left behind a career in order to follow Me. Because of your obedience I am going to anoint you to free people from bondage. Do not be afraid because I will prepare you ahead of time for those I will send for ministry. As you pray for them and get stronger, I will send harder cases to you, but all the while I will be preparing you for the task. Do not go out and try to find people to pray for. I will send them to you as I see you are ready for them."

During the next several months as a dialysis nurse, I took my Berean Bible School courses to work, and my dear Christian patient "went to school" with me while her blood was being filtered.

Finally I had to tell her why I would soon be leaving her. She wasn't surprised, because I was studying Bible courses with her. She was already aware that our parting was going to be soon.

Home Bible Study Group

Parallel to this, at our Friday night Bible study, more people were coming to our home group, giving both my husband and I opportunities to share what God was teaching us.

What were we learning? Spiritual warfare. Just like Jesus told His apostles: "Heal the sick, raise the dead, cleanse those who have leprosy, drive out demons. Freely you have received, freely give" (Matthew 10:8). God had set me free of rejection and fear, and delivered Ken from the spirit of blasphemy. Now He wanted us to do likewise: to study and learn how to free others who were in bondage to demonic strongholds.

So we did. We studied the Bible. We went to seminars. I picked the brains of our church's own resident deliverance minister, Rev. Fran Harrison. We listened to tapes. Then, after a year of meeting every Friday night, we decided to share a tape series on deliverance with the group, telling them that after six weeks of these tapes, we might be ready to pray for someone who was in bondage.

One man approached Ken and said he couldn't wait. He said, "Ken, I have a spirit of fear. It is jeopardizing my job. Will you cast it out of me? I can't get out of bed in the morning without a battle. Will you cast the fear demon out of me?"

That was the beginning of our deliverance ministry. Cars would be parked all over the streets every Friday as people came for help. Addicts were delivered;

homosexuals were set free from their perverse desires. Jesus gave us a new life and now He was using us to help others find peace, freedom and joy again.

Eventually Ken was ordained, and I became a licensed minister.

Heresy?

After we were in full-time ministry, we knew that we should be under the authority of a respected ministry group, but we couldn't be ministers in the Assembly of God because we had been divorced. So we joined United Evangelical Churches, based in Thomasville, Georgia.

Not long after joining, we heard that our superior was coming to pay us a visit, because reports were coming in to him that we might be dangerous. He came with his wife to observe us. He felt a responsibility to protect people from our contamination, and had come to check us out.

They stayed in our home and attended the Sunday evening service at Lakeland's First Assembly of God. The only seating available in the church was on the front row.

God takes care of His kids! Our pastor, Karl Strader, normally would read small testimonies of a line or two from a prayer card. That night, however, when Brother Hardin was there checking up on us, pastor read a six-page letter from a woman who had previously had a prolapsed mitral valve and life-threatening arrhythmias. She had been in and out of intensive care for the last several years and had already arranged for the care of her children after her death. She had been waiting to die.

She shared in her testimony how she had come to our deliverance service and the spirit of death left her, in the name of Jesus, and now she is working with her husband in his lawn care business doing heavy physical work.

The doctor checked her over and couldn't find anything wrong with her heart anymore. When our visitors heard this, they were quite startled. I just praised God!

Healing

The following night he was at our typical deliverance service. We paid no special attention to him and his wife. We just taught like we teach and prayed like we pray, and God healed him of a lifelong back problem, totally and completely. Jesus also restored his wife in a painful emotional area. Praise the Lord.

Brother Hardin was so happy with the ministry that, instead of removing us from the fellowship, he told us that he had heard from God. "Next year's conferences for all the ministers and missionaries will be focused on spiritual warfare as the topic," he said. God also told him that Ken and Nancy Curtis were to open both conferences, the one in California and the one in Memphis, with a deliverance service.

Charles Hardin knew that his ministers needed deliverance. They also needed to learn about spiritual warfare. Praise God!

I want to tell you that attacks may come as you walk along the way. Some of them may come from within your new Christian environment. But God is on your side. No weapon formed against you will prosper. Hallelujah. The battle is the Lords! (2 Chronicles 20:17-29)

This could have been an intimidating experience for an ACoA. Yet, when one is yielded to the Holy Spirit, we can be filled with peace that passes understanding and just keep going. God will take care of changing the hearts of accusers or judges. Just relax.

All the board members were required to attend the conference. Some of the most precious moments we have ever experienced were when these men approached Ken, and with tears streaming down their faces, hugged him. They told him how much they loved him and how they were sorry they had been so critical. God had touched them and restored them that day. They just wanted to thank us and tell us they were sorry.

Harlem, New York City

Less than five years after our back-porch beginnings we were invited to minister in a tent on a field in Harlem, New York.

I had never been to New York, and I had some very prejudiced opinions of it. As our airplane came in over the tall buildings, before it landed at La Guardia, I peeked out of my window at the size of the city and got nauseated.

After we had picked up our baggage, we waited for our ride to show up, and no one came. So this "formerly fearful female" jumped into a cab with my husband, and we told the driver to let us off in front of the tent in Harlem. (We later found out that cabs were not taking passengers into that neighborhood, so God must have motivated our driver and protected us.)

For the next three days we lived in a sixteen-foot camper that was parked in the field near the crusade tent. Water was brought in five-gallon jugs from the corner fire hydrant. The fence around the field had no gate, and the camper had no lock on its door. I was the only white female spending the nights on the premises. We had three men volunteering as security personnel.

When we are doing what God wants us to do, He gives us the protection we need. Also, if I hadn't been delivered from a spirit of fear, I never would have been able to serve the Lord among the beautiful people of Harlem.

The deliverance services were super. Many came off the streets to our meetings and were delivered from addictions, the occult and rejection from much abuse. They were precious folks and were hungry for knowledge, willing to go back to their homes to cast the demons out of their houses and minister to their loved ones.

Almost

I almost had a problem with fear the second night while we were sleeping in the camper. The ninety-five-degree temperatures had made the people in the neighborhood restless, and a gunfight started on the street next to our camper. I could hear the shots—a couple of bullets hit something. That is when I said, "Ken, are you *sure* that God told you to bring me here?"

Apart from that moment of anxiety I felt a complete peace the whole time we were there.

Later I discovered why. Back home many intercessors were praying for our protection, and because of their prayers, I could wander around Harlem feeling total peace.

As a result of prayer, we made it safely through a difficult assignment. As a result, many more lessons were learned about how the devil uses the same patterns in various cultures. And Jesus sets free those who are in bondage, no matter if it is in Lakeland, Florida, or Harlem, New York.

Depending on Him

A year later, in a small North Carolina town, I was feeling very weary after a long summer of traveling and seminars. This was the third day of our last seminar of the season. A woman approached me at the end of a teaching session. I had announced that the deliverance would be that night, and she was crying.

"I guess I'll have to keep my demons the rest of my life because I have to go home now."

Her husband was an alcoholic. (Most ACoA's marry one to recreate childhood situations, subconsciously hoping to relive their childhoods and "fix" them.)

I had no feelings of human compassion because I was totally drained from our heavy ministry schedule. I was even tempted not to pray, but the Holy Spirit prompted me to pray for her.

Totally dry-eyed and unemotional, I ministered to her. I held her as she wept convulsively. Ten minutes later, as she sat there transformed and at peace, she told me she had never *felt so loved in her whole life!*

I knew that love wasn't my human love. I had none to give. It was Jesus' love she felt as I had obediently yielded, allowing God to use me to heal her. That was as neat for me as it was for her. It was an important lesson, not only for me, but for burned-out parents and ministers as well.

Hope

It was through the testimonies of the people we have helped, along with what the Bible teaches, that I saw how the demonic profile of alcoholism and addiction is repeated over and over again. Because of the years of ministry to tens of thousands of people, I can offer you hope. No one who is addicted to any substance, or who has been hurt and abused by an addict, has to remain in that bondage or that pain. Jesus' name is above all other names, and it is in the name of Jesus that all demon's have to flee.

Sally

Sally came to her first deliverance service with her mother. Addicted to cocaine and alcohol, she was determined to commit suicide that night. Her mom made her come.

That night was the beginning of a new life for her. It didn't happen all at once, but the demon that wanted to kill her left her that night. Soon after, as she continued to faithfully attend the services each week, she was delivered from her addictions. She was hungry for knowledge and thankful that there was a place to go so she could learn how to beat up the devil rather than let him beat her up.

This woman read her Bible, listened to the tapes we recommended and read books to help her understand spiritual warfare. Soon she was no longer a hostage to her addicted estranged husband. His demons couldn't cause her any more pain or keep her jumping like a puppet.

Now she is a minister herself and has been teaching and ministering deliverance in a nearby city for several years. We refer people to her with confidence, because she is fully committed to Jesus Christ.

Divine Intervention

Alcoholism and all the related profiles and supporting structures, like denial, are demonic forces. For those of us who were sinned against by the addict there is hope. Some have been suffering for a long time from our reaction to another person's sins.

You have seen in this book a host of classic ACoA characteristics. They are actually demonic drives and bondages that can be dealt with supernaturally by the power of God, once one admits that he needs help. Even secular AA leaders acknowledge that divine intervention is needed for real recovery.

Just as we have seen thousands of lives changed as a result of simple teaching and the power of God setting them free, so can yours be changed without you having to spend years in a counseling office.

That is why we wrote our first book, *Tormented?... God's Keys To Life*. This book can now be found in most Christian bookstores. It is a simple, concise, step-by-step training manual on spiritual warfare. Each week we get letters from different parts of the world testifying that after reading the book, they were able to pray and be set free from the oppression in their lives.

In fact, a few weeks ago a woman approached me when we were ministering in New York. She told me that four years earlier she bought our first book. At that time she was dying of cancer and her seven-year-old son was violent and rebellious. There was no one around her who could help her, she said.

She read the book, prayed as instructed in the book, and God healed her of cancer and delivered her son. With a grin on his face, he stood at her side as she related these miracles to me. He agreed that he felt great. Praise God!

Missionary After All

Forty-one years have gone by since God first asked me to sell out and serve Him. I guess I am a missionary now. We've prayed for people from Harlem to Barbados, from Washington State to North Carolina. The book we wrote is being used on the mission field in various places around the world and in Sunday schools.

It's never too late. I want to encourage you that no matter what you have done in your life, no matter what you are still doing, you can become all you were meant to be. You can be free.

Let God start the process in your life. It won't be a one-time quick-fix experience. You can see, as you read this book, that God restores us at the pace that He knows is best for us.

Some Christians call this process, sanctification. Others, like us, see it as getting delivered of evil spirits that produce ungodly fruit in our lives.

It took a while before God's circumstances caused me to face another demonic stronghold in my life, because of one of the roles Satan seduced me into adopting as a child.

Would you believe gall stones were the catalyst for my freedom?

CHAPTER EIGHTEEN

Exposing Wrong Motives

Why did I wait? Ten years earlier they were seen on a routine x-ray. The children teased me mercilessly about the burping and gas. I grew more dependent on taking laxatives.

A most embarrassing situation was at hand for a person in a ministry of healing and deliverance. How could a person who is used by God to heal other people submit to a surgeon? Wouldn't that be denying the healing power of God that we were proclaiming each week? When the stones were first discovered I went for prayer, believing that God would heal me.

As the years passed, I believed that the stones were gone, or could it be that I was denying that they were still there? When the symptoms were interfering with my life, a fever of one-and-a-half years' duration along with pain and indigestion, I went for another checkup. The stones were still there.

God's Intervention Again

Meanwhile, God was getting my attention in other ways regarding this situation. Every conference and seminar where we ministered had someone missing because of gallbladder surgery. We also stumbled across several articles about ministers who had to alter their plans because of emergency gallbladder surgery. At the same time, God had arranged to have my eldest daughter working on the liver transplant floor at a great hospital. She was telling me stories of the repairs they often had to do because of botched up emergency gallbladder surgery.

No longer could I avoid facing the inevitable. If God, for some unknown reason was not going to heal me through prayer, then I would have to have an operation. Knowing that Satan could use this situation to hurt the ministry, there was no way that I was going to take a chance on having an emergency situation and have surgery in some strange city, in the middle of the night, by a tired doctor that I didn't know.

Our intercessors had already been praying and seeking the Lord's guidance regarding this matter. They advised me to quietly seek medical help in another city and not to tell anyone, because of the local opposition to our ministry, especially by satanists. My own doctor was giving me a hard time and was telling me to live with the problem. Then, at the next appointment, I very firmly told him that I was going to go to the city where my daughter worked and have the gallbladder removed. He finally agreed that it was the right thing to do, because walking around with stones that could get stuck was like walking around with a time bomb. He also admitted that he had personal reasons for being against the surgery, and they were related to problems that his dad experienced.

I know that the change in the doctor's attitude was the result of prayer, but I was still having an inner struggle, not with pain, but with *why?*

Why?

Why, God, do I have to have surgery? You have healed thousands of people before my eyes, why not me? I know that all things work together for good. You taught me that years ago. I need to know what You are trying to teach me through this situation.

So we set aside a few weeks out of our travel schedule, and I drove to Atlanta. Ken was planning to fly up and join me for the operation and then fly back home. I did not want this situation to disrupt Spiritual Warfare Ministries. Then I would have guilt to contend with, too.

By then I was looking forward to being pampered for a little while. Three of my children lived in Atlanta: two daughters (both nurses) and a son who is a senior art director with an ad agency. I would be staying with my girls after the surgery. In fact, the reason I was able to get into this hospital was because my girls were nurses there. One had chosen the surgeon for me, because he was the most skilled doctor she knew on the liver-transplant floor.

Everything was perfect—loving children, super doctor, superior hospital—then why was I feeling so scared? Fear was one of the first problems that I overcame, I thought, after I became a Christian. Something was wrong. The night before the operation I was demanding reassurance from the anesthesiologist that everything would be all right. Even my EKG was abnormal.

Dear Lord, what is wrong with me? I'm in the best situation I could be in and I'm scared. God, please show me the reason for all this.

I tried reading my Bible, but was unable to comprehend what I was reading. This feeling of helplessness was making me miserable. What was going to happen tomorrow? Was someone going to make a mistake. Was I going to die?

Ken came and slept next to my bedside. Morning came quickly and they came for me earlier than expected. The next twenty-four hours are a foggy memory.

I do remember hurting and being totally self-centered. Looking back, it's like going through stages of development like a baby. First of all, the world revolved around me. Then I gradually became aware of those around me, and started becoming considerate of their schedules.

Feeding me ice chips was one way Ken tried to help me be comfortable. He spent one more night holding my hand, which meant a lot to me, then he flew back home. His support during my trial really uplifted me.

Recovery

My recovery was miraculous. After the first twenty-four hours I needed no more pain medication. In four days I was discharged. Seven days post-op I was already walking over two miles around hilly Atlanta. Five and one-half weeks after the surgery I was able to hike six miles with a 1,000-foot climb up and down a mountain at an altitude of 5,500 to 6,600 feet, which is like climbing the empire state building up and down again!

The doctor had said that I could walk all I wanted to, but I was not to lift anything heavier than the Atlanta phone book, so I walked and walked. The fever was gone, my digestion was finally working normally, and I had lots of energy with no more "sinking spells" during the day; in fact, more energy than I can remember having in many years.

I used the walking time after the operation to ask God to show me why I had to go through this trial.

He said, "Nancy, do you remember when you had your five children by the Natural Childbirth (no anesthetic) method?"

I said, "Yes, Lord, but what does that have to do with gall stones?"

The Answer

Then the Lord pointed out the connection, the scar, the contamination that was still in my life as a result of growing up in a dysfunctional home.

He said, *"You thought that you had your babies without anesthetic, because you wanted them to have the best start in life possible. That is true, but haven't you noticed how proud you have been of the fact that you were in control in the labor and delivery room?* **You had no choice** *but to be awake when you had your babies because* **you had to be in charge**. *The reason you put off having your gall stones out for ten years was not because you were believing that I would heal you. You procrastinated because you knew that* **when they put you to sleep you would not be in control of the operating room.**"

That was part of the pattern of "having to be in charge" which I picked up as a young girl.

Oh, God, what have I done? I didn't trust the doctors to know what they were doing and ultimately that means that I didn't trust You. I'm sorry, Lord, please forgive me.

Finally I was beginning to find peace about having to have the surgery. Can you imagine, though, how I suffered for ten years because I was still contaminated with the role of the *one who has to be in control at all times.* Because of that, I couldn't face being anesthetized. That meant that I would not be running the show.

By healing me through surgery, God showed me how my life was being distorted by a demonic stronghold. I wouldn't have become aware of this had I not had the surgery. He told me to share this testimony to help others. For me, it was just gallstones, for others, it may be something more serious.

This testimony is already saving lives. After I teach on alcoholism and its results, many people approach me and tell me that my testimony opened their eyes. They will no longer put off seeking the medical intervention they need. My frank admittance of my motives for not having an operation for ten years uncovered hidden denial and fear in their lives. With that discovery they are then set free to get the help they need.

A Lighter Lesson in Trust

While recuperating in Atlanta I looked in the mirror one day and decided that my shaggy hair looked awful. I don't know how you are, but when I finally find a hairdresser that I trust, it is very hard for me to go to anyone else for fear of ending up looking awful.

But in this city, I had to take a chance with a stranger. My daughter told me to go to her hairdresser, but that fell through. The next day, while at a mall I was overcome by a moment of boldness and asked a salesgirl if there was a beauty salon in the mall. She told me how to find it.

The lady at the desk reached out and patted my hair and asked me if I would be willing to be a model for them the next morning in exchange for a free haircut. Since I had just learned that I could trust surgeons and anesthesiologists, I decided to be adventurous and return in the morning.

The owner of a string of salons was coming in to teach his hairdressers a certain haircutting technique, and they needed fifteen volunteers for the hairdressers to practice on.

The next morning I arrived with the other "guinea pigs," and we all watched while the "boss" demonstrated the new cut. Then he told the hairdressers each to pick one of us and get started.

Rejection

Did you ever get left out when sides were being chosen for a team? No one wanted me. They were one hairdresser short, and I was the only one not picked. (The other women had wavy hair, long necks and thin faces.) I can't begin to tell you how awkward I felt standing there alone. Many old demonic feelings started bothering me, and I almost yielded to either walking out or crying. Instead I prayed for favor and walked up to the girl at the desk.

God answered my prayer. The secretary had just found out that the owner of the beauty shops had nowhere to go after this stop. So, instead of having a novice practice on me, my hair was cut by the owner himself! Praise the Lord! Just for fun, I asked him what it would have cost me if I had to pay him, and he said $54. The Bible says the last shall be first and the first shall be last (Mark 10:31).

This story might seem frivolous, but for someone just learning to release control of everything into God's hands, this was a monumental victory. When I leave it up to God and don't yield to the old demonic patterns, He takes care of me better than I would even hope for. When I returned to Lakeland, I had many compliments on my haircut.

Blessed Relief

When the works of darkness are brought to light, they lose their power. I have learned that I can trust God in all things. Through the way He brought me through this season, God showed me that He loves me and will see to it that "all things will work together for good."

Did you ever try to help keep an airplane in the air by holding it up by the armrests? That was me before I was set free!

I learned that I am not supposed to be always in control. Only when I became aware of this could I relax and find peace. What a relief it is.

It takes a monumental amount of energy to run everybody else's show. Perhaps that is one reason I have so much energy now.

CHAPTER NINETEEN

Spiritual Warfare

Before anyone goes to battle, he or she must first recognize there really is a war.

See if you recognize yourself in the following list:

CHARACTERISTICS OF
ADULT CHILDREN OF ALCOHOLICS

Janet G. Woititz, Ed.D., Health Communications, Inc, pp. 59-90, Copyright © 1983; Reprinted by permission.

1. Adult children of alcoholics guess at what normal is.
2. Adult children of alcoholics have difficulty following through from beginning to end.
3. Adult children of alcoholics lie when it would be just as easy to tell the truth.
4. Adult children of alcoholics judge themselves without mercy.
5. Adult children of alcoholics find it difficult to have fun.

6. Adult children of alcoholics take themselves very seriously.
7. Adult children of alcoholics overreact to changes over which they have no control.
8. Adult children of alcoholics constantly seek approval and affirmation.
9. Adult children of alcoholics have difficulty with intimate relationships.
10. Adult children of alcoholics usually feel different from other people.
11. Adult children of alcoholics are either very responsible or very irresponsible.
12. Adult children of alcoholics are extremely loyal, even in the face of evidence that the loyalty is undeserved.
13. Adult children of alcoholics tend to lock themselves into a course of action without seriously considering alternative behaviors or possible consequences. This impulsiveness leads to confusion, self-loathing and loss of control.

Do you see yourself in any of these? Then this chapter will arm you with the weapons you need to conquer many of these areas. The first step is recognizing your real enemy.

Reassurance

Have you ever spent time rehearsing just what you were going to say, and then when you are with the person you find yourself saying things you never intended to and later wish you hadn't said at all?

That is an example of a demon using you. It doesn't matter if it was in you or around you in the room. The point I want to make here is that sometimes demons talk through people. Our problem has been our inability to recognize when that is happening.

The purpose of this book is to help you recognize demonic activity so you can then do something about it.

I am not judging whether or not the person is sinning, nor am I saying these people are demon possessed.

When a person first starts to express a certain ungodly trait, it may be that he is just succumbing to temptation. It is after some time passes that the person is no longer able to choose what he is saying in certain situations, it is a demon talking through him.

Diseases Don't Talk, Demons Do

A new model has been proposed in this book. It is not a disease talking, it is a demon talking. As I said before, did you ever hear a disease talk? Did you ever hear tuberculosis talk? diabetes talk? or cancer talk?

Spirits of TB, cancer, diabetes and other diseases are capable of talking. When confronted during deliverance we have heard them say, "I won't leave her." "She is mine." "I will kill him." "Please don't make me go." "I'll get you if I leave him."

You probably heard a spirit of self-pity talking as the demon in the victim of the disease expresses its depression and feelings, or you may have heard the spirit of anger talk as a sick person "ventilates" his feelings about the situation. Perhaps it was the spirit of depression or the spirit of grief. Notice I am saying these are spirits talking.

Remember, Jesus had to turn to Peter one time and say, "Get behind me, Satan." That was because a demon spoke through Peter's mouth.

What do we sometimes do in life? Our own words, and our language belies our inner awareness of spirit beings. You and I are spirits, we live in our bodies and we have souls. I am Nancy, I am a spirit and I live in this body.

This body is my earth suit. I have a soul. My soul is my mind, will and emotions. I am a spirit, created by God. Now, my soul (my mind, will and emotions) and my body are areas where Satan can attack and demons can operate.

Spirits can go through walls and solid objects, so let's not get hung up with terminology like possession, obsession and all those semantics.

But right now we will present a short course in spiritual warfare.

I, Nancy the spirit, gave my life to Jesus Christ. I am born again, saved, and I'm going to heaven, if I don't turn away from God, or return to a life of sin and rebellion. But it must be as obvious to you as it is to me that there are many Christians that don't act like Christians should act. That's because in our souls (mind, will and emotions) still remain areas of demonization. These are areas over which we have not yet made Jesus Christ the Lord.

Now if Jesus is really Lord of your tongue, I mean *really* Lord of your tongue, you wouldn't gossip, complain, belittle or lie. If Jesus is *really* Lord of your sex glands, you would not fornicate, masturbate or withhold sex from your spouse. If Jesus is *really* Lord of your stomach (and the Bible has some strong statements about people who have their belly as their god), you would not overeat or feed yourself garbage. (Actually it's demons feeding you garbage, acting perverse and using your tongue.)

Trust

For some unknown reason people have trouble sub-
mitting to God. I'm talking about the flesh, the ego, our
unwillingness to yield. A lot of us, especially those who
have been victims, have never been able to trust God.
Making Jesus Lord of our life and really trusting our lives
and everything about us into His hands is very difficult.
In fact, as I have said before, when we ask for hands to
be raised in our services, more than ninety-five percent
let us know that they have been victims. They are Adult
Children of Alcoholics or victims of dysfunctional
families.

The ministry of deliverance is for people in the grips
of something that is producing sinful behavior, despite
their unwillingness to sin. Other times they are unaware
of it, but those that love them, work with them or live
with them notice those ungodly traits.

One therapist believes that most victims have psycho-
logical problems that need to be worked out, but when
victims have been abused he sees that they can be
demonized.

What do we mean by demonized? The Bible says that
we wrestle not with flesh and blood (Ephesians 6:12),
but with principalities, powers, the rulers of the darkness
of this age, and spiritual wickedness in high places. That
means that you have been in spiritual warfare all of your
life whether you knew it or not. You grew up on a battle-
field, especially if you grew up in an alcoholic home.

Most of us, however, tend to see these unpleasant
encounters with natural eyes.

Invisible Enemies

Now let's look at the ordeals you have been through
with spiritual eyes. You heard horrible things come out

of the mouth of your mother or your dad. You experienced beatings, you heard accusations, you felt rejection, you were told you were stupid, you were told you would never amount to anything. You were told if you would only try harder, or if you would do this or do that, then Daddy or Mommy would be better, be happy, quit drinking, etc.

That was *not a disease talking. Those were demons talking. Every one of your enemies is invisible.*

Understanding this is as essential to your recovery as it was for mine. This is why the Bible was written. All of your enemies are invisible and arranged in different ranks. Some are over territories, countries, communities, or groups of people, like churches and homes (where the spirits of alcoholism, denial and all of their components have been operating through your family line).

Daniel 10:13 gives a vivid illustration of a demon ruling over these territories: "But the Prince of the Persian kingdom resisted me twenty-one days. Then Michael, one of the chief princes, came to help me...."

In this scripture, the "Prince" was a demon ruler over Persia, who resisted the angel coming to answer Daniel's prayers.

So when AA or other groups encourage the alcoholic to reach a "higher power," unless that power is Jesus, they are reaching for more trouble than they had to begin with.

That "higher power" could end up being a demon ruler that reigns in the heavenlies (Ephesians 6:12).

John 14:6 makes it very clear that there is **no other way to God the Father, except through Jesus Christ.**

As Christians we understand that we have millions of enemies, every single one of them is invisible, and they are all demons. That's not scary news. The scary part was being helpless all my life. The good news is that every

Christian has been given authority over all demon powers.

"And these signs will accompany those who believe: In my name they will drive out demons; they will speak in new tongues..." (Mark 16:17).

Don't Fret

Psalm 37 says we are not to fret. Fretting is worrying. Worry is not trusting God. Again, a victim has a hard time trusting. But God's Word is the only authority we have.

Psychologists have about 284 different role models that each school of thought regards as normal. They argue among themselves about which one is the model of a healthy personality.

The Bible shows us our model. Jesus Christ is Perfection. He is the goal, the only direction a human being should go toward, as far as being perfect. That keeps it simple and that is the direction we are trying to attain all of our lives. He is our model. One model, simple model. Read about Him in the Gospels.

When I was a very young Christian, as I saw different family and financial situations coming apart I said, "I can't change anything around me, God, please change my attitude about what's going on around me." That was a little-bitty-baby step of deliverance, because after that prayer I felt different about what was going on around me, and along with it seemed like everybody changed.

It could be that some of you have had breakthroughs like this in your lives. They didn't last for long, did they? You may have thought, oh, wow! I've found the answer, and then you are back facing the same struggles again. Why?

Could it be that you are turned over to the tormentors because of unforgiveness?

Choosing

So many think that they'll be happy when someone wonderful comes along who won't react adversely to their problems. The secret to happiness is not in finding the right person, but in making right choices. You are going to have to choose the directions that you will take.

So you are sick and tired of being sick and tired? Of being a victim over and over again? Victims attract people who abuse and take advantage of them.

Depression or frustration are just symptoms of a deeper problem. If you pluck a leaf off a tree, another one comes back. The leaves must be dealt with by destroying the roots of the tree. So it is with symptoms. The root of depression, frustration, etc. must be destroyed.

We're going through a process to get the roots out. Right now you may or may not be aware of the roots of your pain, it depends on what stage of recovery you are in. But hopefully you are fed up with certain behavior patterns that have plagued you most of your life. You don't want this to continue down through your children and their children. So decide now, OK, that's it.

With great willpower people have done wonderful things, like quitting smoking. I used my will to stop being crabby. I knew it was a sin to be crabby.

I'm part Irish, and with all the children in the house there was a lot of noise and activity. When I realized it was wrong to scream and fly off the handle, I quit doing it. At that time I was newly married to Ken and there was a lot of change in our home since our combined families had eight children between eleven and eighteen years old. I decided not to get mad anymore.

Strange Remedy

I'd open a bedroom door and see the chaos, and I would sigh. Then I'd walk into the kitchen and see the dirty dishes and sigh, or go outside and see the unweeded garden and sigh. Then I would see the financial disaster, and I would sigh. I was really good—I quit sinning. I made myself, by the sheer act of my will, quit sinning.

What did I do? I sighed for three months. I didn't get mad, I suppressed it. Do you know what happened? There was still a spirit of anger in me. Did you ever hear that buried resentment makes you sick? The Bible says so, and medical science says so.

I didn't get mad anymore. I didn't sin anymore. I'm telling you this to let you know that just making a decision to stop feeling some way or doing something is not necessarily going to lead to your recovery. What happened to me? I started getting weaker and weaker. I woke up in the morning feeling like a dishrag, and I went to work as a dialysis nurse feeling weak and shaky. Finally, I felt so bad that Ken took me to a well renowned cardiologist. He looked at me, listened to me describe my problem, opened his cabinet and gave me a pile of brown paper bags. My problem was that I was hyperventilating!

That was definitely an act of God, getting me to the right doctor and giving that doctor wisdom. Remember, when you yield your life to the Lord, He will get you pointed in the right direction. Trust Him.

The doctor gave me those bags and told me to get up in the morning and take twenty breaths with the bag over my face. I was to do this often during the day. I had breathed in so much extra oxygen over the past several months that I had changed the pH of my blood. I did not have enough carbon dioxide in my blood, and I had to rebreathe in a paper bag to get the carbon dioxide level restored. It was the most amazing thing. After just a "day on the bag" I felt instantly better.

I was embarrassed, too. The world had taught me to "go ahead and express anger so you don't get sick." But the Bible has a different solution. I was repressing that anger. (It wasn't my anger, it was a trespasser, a demon. Often when we tell those demons to go they talk back and they say, "This is my house." But they often say it in a different voice than the person's voice. Remember that. These "things" are trespassers, they do not belong there. It is not their house.) But this anger spirit was still there, even though I was not expressing it.

(The bag experience was good training for us in our ministry, too, because now we watch out for hyperventilating in our deliverance services. When we see signs of hyperventilation we just simply tell them not to breath so hard. If they are not cooperative, we give them a bag because it would not be right to give the devil credit for cramped fingers and a tingling feeling when the person was just hyperventilating while trying so hard to be set free. The demon is just trying to confuse them.)

What I'm trying to tell you is that just wanting to stop certain behavior is not going to necessarily make you better. It's going to pop up in another area, like high blood pressure, migraine headaches, and other health problems. You may have already experienced that. You can will to stop sinning and stop, but if you have the demon in you that caused that sinful behavior, then you could end up sick from the inner turmoil of those suppressed emotions. When the demon is cast out, the accommodating evil activity, emotions and desires leave you along with the evil spirit. You no longer have to suppress it. The urge to sin in that area is gone, along with the demon.

Forgive

When you forgive, you tear up an IOU. God says, "Vengeance is mine, I will repay." The Lord is telling you to tear up that IOU. That means it is just as if it didn't happen. You're not going to feel any immediate rush of wonderful love toward the person you had to forgive, but the restoration of your emotions is beginning.

Restoration

God will begin restoring your emotions *after* you forgive. Then peace will come. I'm not talking about pretending or denial. A grin-and-bear-it attitude, or one of stoicism, is not the same as complete release and freedom.

As a child you weren't able to forgive the person who abused you. You were hurt and scared. It is very important at this point to also bring to your attention the need to forgive the person upon whom you depended for protection from harm, and didn't. He or she let you down and didn't protect you, or didn't believe you when you told what was happening.

If your mother did not protect you from a molester, you need to forgive her too, because she let you down, really let you down. But she also was blinded by demonic powers and did not really know what he or she was doing.

Satanic High Priestess Delivered

The disk jockey on the radio was requesting prayer for a fifteen-year-old girl who was running for her life. For several days, Mary had been calling the station and the prayer line for help, saying that a coven of witches was after her. I was called for advice during this time, so I felt involved, even though I had never met the girl. I certainly was praying for her safety.

On that Friday night our church had a Debby Boone concert and I received another call that they had the witch that had been hunting the girl, in the radio station. A team of prayer warriors had been ministering to her for hours and it looked like she was receiving some deliverance, but they were all exhausted and would I please come and help.

I dressed quickly and got there around 11:00 p.m. She (I'll call her Carol) was sitting on the floor and there were about fifteen people around the radio studio praying and watching. As soon as Carol saw me she opened her purse and popped some pills into her mouth and uttered an obscenity. I sat down next to her and started to read Psalm 91 out loud, putting her name in it; eg., Carol is dwelling in the secret place, etc. Near the end of the Psalm she suddenly got up and tried to escape. The hallway was round, so she couldn't find the exit in her confused state. She ducked into the main broadcasting room where the song, "Can You Reach My Friend" was playing. There she slumped into a chair and started to cry.

Then I made my next move. God had given me a word of knowledge about why she had gotten into satanism. I wrote it down and handed it to the man in charge of her deliverance. He read, "You have been let down by your mother who didn't protect you from sexual abuse, and that is why you have become involved in the occult."

She lunged at him and said, "How did you know?" Then she started crying and coughing as we rebuked the demons of hate and rebellion.

Another Identity

Carol had admitted that the girl who had been calling the radio was she. So, it looked like Carol had been using the name Mary and an identity of a fifteen-year-old to harass the radio studio.

But now the power of God was making a difference in Carol's life. As midnight approached (she was to be on the other side of town at midnight to become the bride of some demon at a satanic ritual), she cried out that they would just patch her in if we didn't let her go. The deliverance team continued to discern spirits and cast them out of Carol until, at 2:00 a.m., Carol gave her life to Jesus.

The next day she received more ministry and on Sunday she walked to the altar and made a public profession of her Christianity. Then Carol was taken into the home of the disk jockey and his wife. We saw her in the office and ministered to her some more. Ken arranged for her to go to Teen Challenge, since she had been a high priestess in satanism and really needed an environment that would provide safety and expert continuous support for her Christian growth.

Before she went there she returned to her parents to tell them she was all right. Then she went to her home in Atlanta, only to find that the satanists had burned it down. (That took care of her need to destroy all her satanic artifacts.) The coven she came out of even mailed her the hand of another satanic high priest with his ring still on his finger—this was a warning of what they would do to her.

Discernment

At Teen Challenge the leaders were concerned because she wasn't acting like a Christian. (By the way, now she was using a third name—Judy.) So Judy was not acting like she was saved. Suddenly the disk jockey who had been helping her realized that Judy had never given her life to Jesus. Carol did. Carol was just the name of a demon. Mary, the fifteen-year-old, was a demonic personality too.

What happened? The demon calling itself Carol mouthed the sinners prayer to let everyone think that they had led someone to Jesus. The real person, Judy, still hadn't surfaced. It was only after much more ministry that Judy was uncovered. Judy had never, of her own will, given her life to Jesus.

So the personnel at Teen Challenge, when they were told this, went to her room and led her to the Lord.

Now she is traveling all over, a transformed person, telling of the wonders of the Christian life. Praise God.

(One of the points I want you to notice in the above testimony, beside the fact that she went into the occult because of her great disappointment in her mother, is that when we are dealing with demons, we often are duped into thinking we are dealing with a human being. *When there are profound personality changes, whether accompanied by different names or not, there probably are demons operating through that person—different ones at different times.* Therefore, if you hear one "personality" make a promise one day, it is quite possible that the "other personality" doesn't know anything about that promise. That fits the profile of an alcoholic too.)

Some parents are starting to become concerned because their children are acting **out of character** after spending a lot of time with certain video games and Dungeon & Dragon type games. What does *out of character* mean? Something else is manifesting through the child. That something else can periodically "take over" a personality when we open the doors to the occult. Read on.

The Occult

I said in the beginning that there is another reason that alcoholism has been coming down your family line. That is occult activity. Deuteronomy 18 lists the curses, some of the things that befall a family that has been involved in occult activity. What do we mean by occult activity?

The first commandment in Exodus 20:2-5 says: "I am the LORD your God, who brought you out of Egypt, out of the land of slavery. You shall have no other gods before me. You shall not make for yourself an idol in the form of anything in heaven above or on the earth beneath or in the waters below. You shall not bow down to them or worship them; for I, the LORD your God, am a jealous God, punishing the children for the sin of the fathers to the third and fourth generation of those who hate me."

Jesus said, "I am the way, the truth and the life and there is no way to the Father except through me" (John 14:6).

If your family line seems to be cursed, you might notice that there are more problems than alcoholism. Maybe poverty is plaguing your family generation after generation also. Possibly incest and insanity and other obsessive-compulsive disorders are being repeated down the family line.

Bondage

There are reasons that we end up cursed. Yes, I mean cursed. We are discussing spiritual warfare. We're not discussing alcoholism as a disease, we are discussing alcoholism as the manifestation of demonic activity. And, along with alcoholism, a whole network of demons are employed in the system with it, including the spirit of denial, which keeps us blind to the source of our dilemma, therefore, in bondage.

Let's say that your great-great grandfather found water with a divining rod. That is a supernatural event. Something made that stick bend. It was a god, a demon. (There are Viking demons, Roman demons, Greek demon gods and goddesses—demons, Egyptian demons and millions of Hindu demon gods.) If we seek another god for healing, guidance, prosperity, or information about the future, we are cursed, and so our our children, our grandchildren and our great-grandchildren.

I'm part Mohawk Indian. There was spiritism and occult activity in my background. Therefore different curses came down the family line. These continued until we broke the power of the devil by renouncing those occult practices and received deliverance. The Bible says the power of life and death is in the tongue (Proverbs 18:21). Occult involvement must be renounced out loud. In front of God and in front of Satan we must say we want nothing to do with it, and mean it. Your will to make a decision has power.

"I will not read my horoscope!" What do horoscopes have to do with the occult? Everything. The god of the horoscopes is not the father of our Lord Jesus Christ. The common occult practices are listed in detail in our other book, *Tormented?*

Searching

Sometime in the past you may have participated in a ritual or ceremony as a scout. Maybe you were initiated into a sorority or fraternity or another secret society. If you look back and do a little research, you will find out that rituals you participated in were duplicating pagan, occultic, witchcraft, or satanic ceremonies and rites.

Our God will not tolerate that. Chants, like mantras for example, are calling and inviting demons into us. We are not to find peace through demons. Our help is in the name of the Lord.

Troubled Traveler

I sat next to a lady in an airplane last week. She was an Adult Child of an Alcoholic, and had gone through a divorce a few years earlier. She was returning back home to see her parents for the first time since she "found her spiritual path" in life.

She looked like she was in her forties and, because of the pain she suffered at the hands of her alcoholic dad, her life came apart and she went on her search for answers, peace and healing. She ended up ensnared in the occult, the New Age.

She had black artificial toenails with silver stars on them, and wore a long baggy dress. Around her neck dangled a weird charm, while she nervously fingered a crystal in her palm.

When we flew through some turbulence, she folded her hands in a strange manner on her lap and meditated. I prayed and asked God to help me and give me wisdom, because the poor girl was confused.

Later I had the opportunity to witness to her on the flight. I shared my testimony, and she is going to buy our book, *Tormented?* I let her know that I was once at the same point she was, and I knew what she was walking through.

I shared with her about what Jesus did for me.

You, too, in your search could have fallen into traps along the way because most of the literature for ACoA's is devoid of any Christian input as yet. And some of the support groups are contaminated with the occult.

A Relative

A person I know well, formerly an atheist, realized that she was helpless to battle alcoholism in her or her husband's life. She too is an ACoA, grew up attempting to be strong, but this battle was wearing her out. It was too much and she realized it. She joined AlAnon, and just six months later, became involved in astrology and metaphysics. She was lured into a metaphysical church in the area.

She is so happy that she doesn't have to be in charge of her life any more, because she has yielded it to a higher power. She doesn't know that her substitute for atheism is demons.

I've tried to witness to her. She knows our beliefs. But there is a lot of power in those groups when one has come to depend on leadership that has "been there." At the present she is ensnared. We are praying for her, and I, too, am trying to love her into the kingdom, instead of condemning her. She has asked me what I think, and I have told her.

But she, like so many of you, suffered as a young person at the hands of insincere Christians. After growing up in church and being a very active participant, she had a crisis in her life. The pastor and everyone else abandoned her. Atheism took its place.

A young man at our service last week shared that he had been trained in Martial Arts and, as a Christian, he wanted to be delivered of all the demons he had invited into himself to receive supernatural strength. He knew those were demons that he acquired, even before we did our teaching on the occult.

As we minister, we often encounter people like my acquaintance and the young man. So many people, after they have been let down by their moms and dads, and then are rejected by their church, go into the occult to have some power so they can finally manipulate their environment.

I understand this reaction, but you must see that when you get further down that path of deception, you are going to be in worse shape than you ever were when people sinned against you.

What Demons Do I Pray Against?

Demons are called by the names of the symptoms they produce. The Bible says by their fruit you will know them. You don't have to use fancy names like you may have heard about in occult circles. When you pray, they will go when you tell them to go calling them by the name of the symptom they cause. Praise God.

After Deliverance, What Next?

After one gets delivered from a spirit of poverty, for example, what does he do next? Like a spiritual Chapter XI, (the bankruptcy proceeding where the creditors are kept off of the back of the debtor while he gets his act together), the next thing to do is get educated. Get some Christian information on financial planning and money handling. Pick some good brains like Larry Burkett's, and fill that gap with good information. **Every time we are delivered of something we must fill that area with the Holy Spirit and God's Word**, and get some sound information.

A person delivered of a spirit of gluttony, a compulsive disorder often found in Adult Children of Alcoholics, often is delivered of spirits of rejection, denial, frustration, and self pity. But he or she may never have learned how to cook anything except southern-fried chicken, gravy, corn, fried okra or other fattening foods. If the person does not get re-educated, he might be free of the spirit but will stay fat and sick, and maybe get discouraged and allow the demons to come back. It is important to get new cookbooks and new information on nutrition. Then with the word in your heart and new information in your head you will be restored.

Then God will deal with other areas of our lives when He sees that we are ready. It's not all going to happen at once. Even if you are delivered of just one spirit, like fear, it's going to make such a profound difference in your life that it will seem like more happened to you than just that. That's how it was with me.

In order to stay free, **read the Word of God daily.** Plead the blood of Jesus when you are being harassed and realize that you have authority over all demonic power in the name of Jesus. Tell any troublesome spirit to go.

A true Christian has authority over all enemy power and can tell it to go in the name of Jesus.

Regrouping

When Jesus forgave a sinner He said to go and sin no more. That person was free and relieved for a while, but he was expected not to sin anymore. A person who is finally free of all this demonic harassment finally has a clear mind. He's able to read the Bible without falling asleep. He can hear from God, get wisdom from God, and pray without coming to a dead end in two minutes. It's easier when one is free from so much demonic activity.

If we do not or will not get our act together, if we prefer to have a predictable bleak future rather than the unpredictable adventure of trusting God, if we are willing to trust God and enjoy the neat adventure of having change in our lives, if we're tired of being victims, we will be more than survivors. We will be more than conquerors through Christ Jesus.

During the time of your spiritual Chapter XI get organized. God will get the creditors, the demons, off of your back. Then use that time and get organized. Get the recipes, the financial information or the sexual counseling that you need from Christians. (At our church, the counseling department likes to send their "special" cases to our deliverance services before they even try to counsel them. That way they don't waste so much time trying to decipher whether they're dealing with a demon or the person.)

How Do I Get Them Out?

You can pray along with us from this book, or *Tormented?* our first book. We also have tapes you can order (see back of book), or come to one of our weekly deliverance services in Central Florida. Another option is to call our offices to find out when we will be in your part of the country.

One woman wrote us to share that she bought a tape of our service and her husband listened to it. She said that after hearing the tape he came downstairs a different man. As a result, the whole family was restored, even the son's girlfriend was saved and filled with the Holy Spirit that week.

There are tapes available of the teaching and deliverance services. The anointing of the Holy Spirit flows through the tapes. Sit down, with either of our books or a tape, and a Bible (be alone; go to the woods if you have to). If you want to be free in some area, and you have forgiven others, gotten rid of the occult bondage in your life, and repented of past and present sins, then pray:

You foul spirit of fear, I bind you, in the name of Jesus! You leave me now, in Jesus' name.

It will go.

Why do we bind the demons first? Because the Bible says, "How can you enter a strong man's house unless you first bind the strong man, and then you can spoil his goods."

When we bind the spirits, which we as Christians have authority to do, then they don't give us so much trouble when they leave. We have learned that through much experience.

Example

A truck driver who wanted to quit smoking saw that his wife was delivered of the spirit of nicotine, and she had quit smoking. He really wanted to stop, so his wife told him, "Sam, you are a Christian and the desire to smoke is only a demon. You can tell that demon to go in the name of Jesus."

He went into the bathroom and did that. Later he shared with us that the desire to have cigarettes left him with a cough. He threw out the cigarettes and never desired one again.

Many people who have quit smoking have testified that it felt to them as if a demon was inside desiring the cigarette. They didn't want to smoke. They were right. It was a demon living inside. The word demon sounds horrible to some folks, but we need to face the truth, because then we can defeat it.

Spirit is *pneuma* in the Greek. *Pneuma* means "breath." So an evil spirit leaves with a breath.

You simply tell the spirit of fear to get out in the name of Jesus. Then just breathe it out. It is as simple as that.

Patience

I know that one of the fruits of the Holy Spirit is patience, but I could not wait for things. I just didn't have any patience. I didn't understand it. I would pray, "Oh, please Lord, give me patience." I would cry out to Him in the morning while I was jogging.

God answered me, "Nancy, you wonder why you are having such a struggle? That is because there is no room for patience; you are so full of *impatience*."

Have you ever said, "I'm full of anger or full of hate?" or, "hate rose up in me?"

What rose up in you? Hate. Was it a feeling? More than a feeling, it was a demon—a demon that expressed that feeling through you. That is how I was with impatience. Full of it.

So, while I continued running along I said, "Impatience, I bind you in the name of Jesus. You spirit of impatience, you go. Leave me right now in Jesus' name." It left. My life then changed *in that area*.

Try doing that sometime with insomnia, if you wake up in the middle of the night, and you are not awake to pray for someone. (You can find that out by praying for whoever you are aware of when you wake up, and you will fall asleep after you are finished praying for that person.) Sometimes, though, I find myself wide awake and not at all feeling spiritual or prayerful. I realize then that I am just getting harassed, and I just say, "I bind you, spirit of insomnia. You leave me right now in the name of Jesus."

It doesn't matter if it is in the room or if it is in me. I tell it to go in the name of Jesus and plead the blood of Jesus over me and the room. When I do that I usually yawn and am sleeping again in a few minutes. I often don't realize until the next morning that I was asleep immediately after rebuking the demon. It's neat!

CHAPTER TWENTY

Condensed Transcript From a Teaching Service: ACoA's

— In Summary —

We talk about Adult Children of Alcoholics and the spirit of denial that has its fingers in many ears already. "My parents weren't alcoholics," or "They weren't really addicts," or "He wasn't really an addict to valium."

Let me share a definition with you. **An alcoholic is someone who drinks, has trouble with his health, finances, relationships or job, and continues to drink.** That is it. The old definition of alcoholism is describing late-stage alcoholism, twenty-five years later. The person is already in bondage to a substance, if he continues to use that substance, whether it be legal or illegal, after he has had problems with his job, relationships, money or health.

So if any of you are related to anyone who has had

223

trouble in any of those areas, has abused any kind of substance, listen carefully.

When I was a little girl, I made a decision. I was tired of going up the streets with my little brother, and looking in the tavern windows because we were hungry. It was Sunday and we wanted dinner, but we couldn't find my parents. So when I was very young, I made several decisions.

One of them was **when I grow up I'm never going to be like my mother!** That was because when I looked around, I did not like what I was experiencing, and I wasn't going to be that way to my kids.

*I wasn't like my mother when I grew up, **I was much worse.***

Why?

Matthew 7:1 warns us not to judge, criticize and condemn others—when you are five, ten, twenty, forty or sixty years old—do not judge so that you may not be judged, criticized and condemned yourselves. Just as I judged my mother, and criticized and condemned my mother, I was judged and criticized and condemned. And in accordance with the measure I used to deal out to her, I was dealt with.

What happened to me? Why do the sins of the fathers come down one more generation? Because I judged. That is a form of unforgiveness. I was turned over to the tormentors, according to Matthew 18. I didn't only drink, but I was hooked on amphetamines for three years when I had little babies in diapers; and I got into a lot of other stuff, up until at age thirty-five I experienced a mid-life crisis.

So I judged, and I criticized, and I made a decision. I ended up repeating the mistakes and the sins of my parents.

How many times have you found yourself doing exactly what you said you would *never do?*

The world also has a statement that it makes. I heard it when I was little, and I heard it as an adult: *"There is nothing worse than a reformed drunk!"* That's true. There is nothing worse—you know drunks say that, and they say that because they can't stand someone who has quit drinking and comes back and tries to get them to quit drinking.

So I got saved, I found Jesus as my Lord and Savior after my life came apart. After I got saved I didn't quit drinking right away, but when I finally did, that's when my old friends knew that my life had been changed by the power of God.

But I was saved, and I was going to go to heaven. I quit drinking, so I was sober. Isn't that wonderful? But I was still proud, I was still fearful, I was still insecure, I was still judgmental, and I went to tell these people about Jesus and how wonderful it was to not drink.

I talked to my brother and said, "It's so great to wake up every morning sober and not have headaches and hangovers." But my brother saw fear and insecurity, pride and arrogant judging.

I didn't win anybody over. You see, if the devil couldn't get me or you, couldn't stop you from serving Jesus, he'll push you so fast and say, "Hurry up and fix everybody yesterday." What did Paul do after he was saved? He went to the desert for three years to get restored, and then he went and preached the gospel.

Driven

I know we're eager, and we want to see people restored after we've met Jesus and we find His power, His mercy and His love. But we are driven to fix these people due to some of the roles that we chose when we

225

were young, and that drive to restore people is not necessarily the Holy Spirit.

Maybe you were the rescuer in the family (that's the one who runs out to fix everybody quick). What happens with this rescuer, this person who tries to keep peace? He'll love everybody and try to explain what Dad meant to Mom, with the desire to keep peace and to rescue.

The problem is we are killing them with the wrong kind of love. You see, *as long as the addict does not have to experience the results of his behavior, he will have no reason to quit.*

Who Needs Help?

There is another one in the family, and that is the rebellious one. That's the one that has the bad grades and gets in trouble in school. That's the one who probably gets counseling. When we understand spiritual warfare, we know that the addict needs deliverance, and we know that the rebellious kid needs deliverance. But those of us who decided to take charge or keep peace, or those of us who end up as victims or decide to be a clown don't usually get the counseling; but we all still need deliverance.

Grief

When we pray tonight, there are some of you who have lost your childhood. And there has been grief over that loss. Those of us who have grown up in these dys-functional homes couldn't be kids because play meant danger was ahead. We never knew while we were having fun when it was going to turn into something scary. And it is hard to have fun now, too—hard to laugh.

How long has it been since you really cried? The Holy Spirit is going to release that grief.

For your emotions to be restored, sometimes there is going to have to be a period of grieving. I want to make you aware now, because I have been hearing testimonies. After we minister this kind of teaching, you may find in a couple of days that you will be weepier than you normally would be. That does not mean that you are depressed, and it's not a demonic attack. It's a release. Just praise God for it.

Guilt

There is another aspect, a demonic stronghold that's picked up by those who grew up in dysfunctional families. Guilt. God wants you to know it's not your fault. They wouldn't have been different if you were quieter, or if you worked harder. And you do not have to be perfect to be loved. You don't have to hurry up for them to like you. If you kept your room cleaner, Dad probably still would have drunk. And if _____, and if _____, and if _____. You fill in the blank, the Holy Spirit will show you.

Sabotage

There's another way that people get sabotaged after deliverance. In fact, you'll be set free in this area, too. So maybe you're not abusing a substance right now, you and I, but do you know what we tend to be when we've grown up in these homes? **Adrenalin junkies**. You see, in a home where there is a period of peace interrupted by chaos, and then peace and chaos, we get used to this *high of adrenalin*. God has given us a Fight or Flight Syndrome. He put these two adrenal glands on top of our kidneys so that when a bear comes after us we can run away or beat him up.

When you were a little kid, you couldn't run away,

and you couldn't deal with that bear, but the adrenalin surged anyway. Little by little it has been eating away at your health. The adrenalin surge.

Know what happens when you get restored and delivered tonight? You are going to feel kind of flat. We get hooked on that high. You see what happens, we get so used to this high that if our life ends up real peaceful, *we miss the high*. It's just the same as when someone misses the high from a puff of nicotine or a drug. I just want to let you know. You will get used to the peace, it's really neat!

There are different highs you can experience. We climbed a mountain, flew kites and picked blueberries. The Holy Spirit will show you new paths and patterns to follow.

Here is a little book. It has five little chapters (Author Unknown).

Chapter 1

"I walk down the street.
There is a deep hole in the sidewalk.
I fall in.
I am lost. I am hopeless.
It isn't my fault.
It takes forever to find a way out.

Chapter 2

"I walk down the same street.
There is a deep hole in the sidewalk.
I pretend I don't see it.
I fall in again. I can't believe I am in the same place.
But it isn't my fault.
It still takes a long time to get out.

Chapter 3

"I walk down the same street.
There is a deep hole in the sidewalk.
And I see it is there.
I still fall in. It's a habit.
My eyes are open. I know where I am.
It is my fault.
I get out immediately.

Chapter 4

"I walk down the same street.
There is a deep hole in the sidewalk.
I walk around it.

Chapter 5

"I walk down another street."

Jesus will show you new streets, new patterns. When the demons get off your case, you will be able to hear from God and see there is another solution, another way. Yes, you are used to operating in the same way, saying the same thing and feeling the same feelings, like the adrenalin highs. But the Holy Spirit is going to show you a new street and you are going to like it. (Read Philippians 3:13-14.)

Bondage

We are not in bondage to the past. God has not given you a spirit of bondage again to fear, but a spirit of adoption whereby we cry, Abba, Father. No matter what happened in your past, no matter how many generations it's been repeating, after tonight you will have a new beginning. You will not be in bondage to the past. Hallelujah! Jesus is Lord, and there is no other.

Healing

Some of you are remembering things you haven't remembered for a while. A lot of you still have blocked out what really happened because of the pain. Especially the sexually abused ones. But the Holy Spirit can still deal with you. You won't need two years on a psychologist's couch. The power of God will restore your life.

If you want to be free, you will be.

You don't want to be sabotaged anymore.

Don't be afraid to cry.

The joy of the Lord is your strength. Realize you are going to have more energy after this, and think more clearly. God's Word will be more alive to you. So forgive those who have wronged you.

What makes a Christian different from a pagan? We love our enemies. We bless those who curse us, and pray for those who spitefully use us. So tonight, remember your real enemies are invisible, they are demons. Forgive all human beings who ever hurt you.

(The above teaching was part of a weekend seminar in spiritual warfare that we did in Tampa, Florida.)

If any of the characteristics in this book describe you, (as they describe many Adult Children of Alcoholics), you don't have to spend anymore of your life in bondage. The following prayer is taken from our book, *Tormented?* You need to find a quiet place to pray.

Notice that in the first part of the prayer, you will be dedicating or rededicating your life to Jesus Christ. There is no other way to real victory except through surrendering your life to Him.

Then, as you have learned, if you **want** to be free, if you have **forgiven**, if you **renounce the occult** and tell God you are **sorry for your sins**, then any ungodly trait, bad habit, compulsion, drive, attitude, evil spirit or demon will leave you, in the name of Jesus, when you *tell it to go.*

Let's Pray

Dear Lord Jesus, I need you. I am sorry for my sins. Forgive me now, and cleanse me with Your Blood.

I give my life to You, dear Jesus, my body, soul and spirit. You are my Lord, my Master, my Savior, and my Deliverer. Thank you, Jesus, for saving my soul! I ask you now, to completely cleanse my body, mind, will, and emotions. Deliver me, Lord, from any stronghold Satan may have in my life because of my sins or those of my ancestors. Deliver me from the tormentors, Lord, that afflict me, because I forgive those who have hurt me.

I lay down all resentment, and I forgive _____ (name them here). And I forgive myself.

Dear Jesus, I want to be sure that Satan's power over me and my family line is completely destroyed. I now renounce, for myself and my ancestors, all dealings with occult powers in any form, and I break all cords of the past, twelve generations back. I am renouncing all witchcraft, sorcery, the New Age, channeling, spiritism, astrology, horoscopes (and my birth sign), ouija boards, fortune telling, palm reading, seances, necromancy, ESP, levitation, transcendental meditation, hypnosis, soul travel, tea leaf reading, automatic handwriting, martial arts, numerology, the pendulum, water witching, spirit guides, curses, charms, fetishes, psychic powers and psychic healing.

I renounce every cult or religion that denies the blood of Christ or the divinity of Christ. I renounce all books, television shows, movies, music, and games that glorify occult practices or experiences.

Through the blood of Jesus, I break all ungodly soul ties and bondages.

I renounce you, Satan, and all your works. You have no place in me and no power over me, through the blood of Jesus. I loose myself from you, in the name of Jesus, and I command you to leave me right now, in Jesus' name.

Thank you Lord for setting me free. Amen.

Now, name out loud what is troubling you the most. If it is fear, say, "Fear, in the name of Jesus, leave me!"

Remember, it is the name of Jesus, the blood of Jesus, and the Word of God that the devil hates. To defeat evil in your life, it is important to memorize scriptures. In this book I testified to the power of the scripture spoken out loud. You can do the same.

After fear goes, tell depression to go. Then rejection, hate, confusion, and so on.

Then spend some time thanking God and praising Him for setting you free and healing you. Ask the Holy Spirit to refill you completely. Then start replacing what left you with the scriptures: read, read, read! Memorize them! Hide them in your heart!

CHAPTER TWENTY-ONE

Answered Prayer

"For a brief moment I abandoned you, but with deep compassion I will bring you back. In a surge of anger I hid my face from you for a moment, but with everlasting kindness I will have compassion on you,' says the Lord your Redeemer. 'To me this is like the days of Noah, when I swore that the waters of Noah would never again cover the earth. So now I have sworn not to be angry with you, never to rebuke you again. Though the mountains be shaken and the hills be removed, yet my unfailing love for you will not be shaken nor my covenant of peace be removed,' says the Lord, who has compassion on you.

" 'O afflicted city, lashed by storms and not comforted, I will build you with stones of turquoise, your foundations with sapphires. I will make your battlements of rubies, your gates of sparkling jewels, and all your walls of precious stones. All your sons will be taught by the Lord, and great will be your children's peace. In righteousness you will be established: Tyranny will be far from you; you will have nothing to fear. Terror will be far removed; it will not come near you. If anyone does attack you, it will not be my doing; whoever attacks you will surrender to you.

" 'See, it is I who created the blacksmith who fans the coals into flame and forges a weapon fit for its work. And it is I who have created the destroyer to work havoc; no weapon forged against you will prevail, and you will refute every tongue that accuses you. This is the heritage of the servants of the Lord, and this is their vindication from me,' declares the Lord" (Isaiah 54:7-17).

Struggling

While walking in the North Carolina Mountains one day, I took along tape recorder. I thought I was going to dictate a chapter for the book, but this prayer came out instead:

> "Lord, I wonder if it was a mistake saying that this book was going to be written. Satan has unleashed forces against me to prevent this book.
> Lord, this is January 30, 1989, and I ask that You protect me. Be a wall of fire around me, especially regarding this book. Protect me from continuous harassment and attack. Seal me off from that attack until the book you want me to do is completed. I'll give You all the credit for the turnaround, for at this point all the chapters seem to be full of self-pity."

Writing this book is really difficult and painful. I don't want to do it. I've put it off, I've tried to quit. I want to write it honestly and truthfully. I'm attempting to face my past honestly, boldly, but it hurts so much to do this. Knowing how God has restored me, it would be so much easier just to be living, and reaching out to others, seeing their lives change. Looking back and writing about my life has caused a demonic attack, making me to feel like I'm still back there at times, just as useless, inadequate and incapable now as I was as a kid.

Praise God, that I still have no desire to drink. I've got the "munchies," and I don't want that. It's still a form of escape. I've prayed and asked for God to give me strength. Like any addict, I cannnot handle it on my own. This problem is too big for me. I've asked God to turn this around, to anoint my writing so it's obvious that the only hope is through Him.

God knows what a dilemma I was in last week. He knows the rejection I was feeling because of the necessity to isolate myself in order to write this book. I've been isolated from any positive input. The only recent memories I've had (besides my husband trying to comfort me, and a few of the staff members we spent a weekend with) are of a harsh phone conversation with my mom.

Then came fresh attacks from the devil.

God knew I was struggling. God also knows what He's doing, even while I write this. I can't write it from an ivory tower to people who are still hurting. Just like the greatest poetry and great songs are written in crises, I've been aware that this book was going to be bought forth in travail. That's probably why I put it off, and had trouble starting it; but since you are reading it, you know that God brought me through the delivery of this book; pulled the book through, more literally.

A Friend

God placed in my heart two desires this week. One was to call a friend who was part of my old beanbag life.

She told me, after a very beautiful conversation, "Nancy, I feel that our friendship is one of God's greatest gifts to me."

Oh, how I needed to hear that.

You have just read how everyone that I knew and every old friend had abandoned me. Now this dear lady, who also has come to know the Lord, is working like I am to restore broken lives of addicts. Although there are miles between us, there is a bond and a love that God has restored.

In the past we had shared some good experiences, too. We didn't just party together. She, like me, wanted to be a better wife. We heard about a "Total Woman" course, and we took it together. We studied it and took it seriously. The course was supposed to transform our husbands, because we would become so neat, submissive and wonderful.

The end of the course has a chapter on how to get the power to do that. There was a prayer, and if I recall correctly, it was a salvation prayer. I mouthed it. I didn't mean it. I didn't even know what it meant. I couldn't comprehend it. Because of that experience I'm aware that some of you and some of those in our audiences may look like they are praying, but it doesn't mean a thing. I've done that, too.

She and I were partners, responsible to call each other and support each other when things were tough. "Total Woman" is a great concept, but when a woman is married to an addict, it makes her a total doormat. We got discouraged. Before a year was up we were simply sucked dry by alcoholism. It didn't help our health or our lives either. The relationship my friend and I had as prayer partners wasn't maintained when all of our lives came apart. She did reach across the gap a few times, but now, what a joy it was to be able to visit with her and to feel the camradery. God knew that. He knew it was right now that I needed that. And I just thank the Lord for it.

God does that for you, too, if you just look real close in your life. There are times when things don't seem to work out, and you try so desperately to learn or do something to patch up your life, or your family or marriage. If it looks like it hasn't worked out yet, believe me, it will.

Everything God is doing in your life is being put together for good. Everything God is allowing in your life is going to develop aspects in you that will cause you to soar over crises in the future. They won't hurt like the ones you remember.

Another Blessing

This week God had kept me restless about a conference here in Lakeland with Marilyn Hickey. For maybe six months I had it marked on my calendar. But when the book writing got so delayed I thought maybe I should skip the conference and just keep writing. So I missed the first night and the second day. The third day I couldn't stand it and kept moving in the direction of going. It was there that a woman who had come to us for help a few years back told me that every time she hears, *Thank You for Giving to the Lord*, by Ray Bowes, she thinks of me and how I had helped her.

When she came to us she was a cocaine addict. We share her testimony elsewhere in this book.

God knows our needs. He will never let us down.

Rejected No More

For me, each day becomes a new adventure toward wholeness. I have not yet arrived at perfection—I'm not even close—nor do I wish to give any false impressions that I am where God wants me to be.

As long as each of us are in this life, we will have to struggle with our own flawed personalities. There is no utopia on this side of heaven, even for those who were blessed with "normal" homes and "normal" parents. At some level, everyone can relate to the principles defined in this book.

I also do not want to leave you with the impression that all of our problems are solved simply by casting out demons. I wish it was that easy. But deliverance can remove the snares that might otherwise hinder your road to recovery.

"Quick fix" solutions don't last—but God's Word firmly placed within your heart will create mental and emotional health for an eternity.

Nancy and Ken Curtis can't always be there for you, as much as we would like to be. You will need a Heavenly Father who never fails, who is responsive to every need.

Several weeks ago as I was completing this book, I found a scripture that touched me at the core of my being. The presence of the Lord rose out of those passages, and I wept profusely as the revelation of His love toward me (and you) was brought forth.

I pray, in closing, that its message will reach out and embrace you with the reality of God's endless love:

" 'On the day you were born your cord was not cut, nor were you were washed with water to make you clean, nor were you rubbed with salt or wrapped in cloths. No one looked on you with pity or had compassion enough to do any of these things for you. Rather, you were thrown out into the open field, for on the day you were born you were despised.

" 'Then I passed by and saw you kicking about in your blood, and as you lay there in your blood, I said to you, "Live!" I made you grow like a plant of the field. You grew up and developed and became the most beautiful of jewels. Your breasts were formed and your hair grew, you who were naked and bare.

" 'Later I passed by, and when I looked at you and saw that you were old enough for love, I spread the corner of my garment over you and covered your nakedness. I gave you my solemn oath and entered into a covenant with you,' declares the Sovereign Lord, 'and you became mine.

" 'I bathed you with water and washed the blood from you and put ointments on you. I clothed you with an embroidered dress and put leather sandals on you. I dressed you in fine linen and covered you with costly garments. I adorned you with jewelry; I put bracelets on your arms and a necklace around your neck, and I put a ring on your nose, earrings on your ears and a beautiful crown on your head. So you were adorned with gold and silver; your clothes were of fine linen and costly fabric and embroidered cloth. Your food was fine flour, honey and olive oil. You became very beautiful and rose to be a queen. And your fame spread among the nations on account of your beauty, because the splendor I had given you made your beauty perfect,' declares the Sovereign Lord" (Ezekiel 16:4-14).

I picked all the fuzz off the Teddy bear.

Dressed for a parade—I played the baritone bugle.

We were a camping
family.

Typical end to a day of boating—being
towed in.

Junior Catholic Symphony Orchestra—I'm the short-haired trombonist.

My five children when life was still simple.

Each of my children won many swim team competitions.

A middle-aged hippie in our beanbag room.

I finally graduated—age 39.

Oh, Happy Day! Ken is mine and I am his.

I met a man who cooked and dyed 6,000 Easter eggs.

Auction Day would have been a major freeze

The last train ride on Auction Day

Camping on the way from Florida to Maryland

Blowout on Washington, D.C. Expressway

Hazel the Bear

A subdued Hazel after her recapture

Assemblies of God dedication at Masterpiece Garden Campground

After the 10,000 meter race

Florida for Jesus

Sharing at Women's Aglow

Ken on a missionary trip to
Sandy Point, Abaco,
Bahamas

Overflow crowd in a South Carolina church

Praising the Lord—Spiritual Warfare Training Conference

TV ministry with Jim Gates of Good Nite Alive

National Geographic interviewed us in the Superdome.

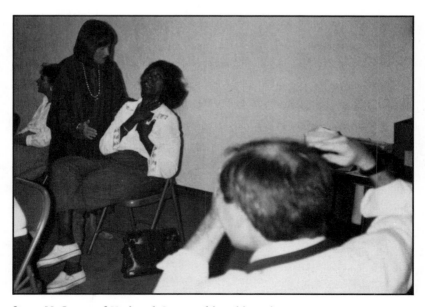

Steve McCurry of National Geographic taking pictures

I climbed up 1,000 feet and hiked 6 miles 5 1/2 weeks after gallbladder surgery.

Golfing with my mother—when she was age 70.

BOOKS AND TAPES ARE AVAILABLE

If you want more information on spiritual warfare and ministry to victims of dysfunctional families, you can order materials by mail or phone.

The following are available:

Tormented?...God's Keys to Life
by Ken & Nancy Curtis......................................$6.00
plus postage and handling.................................$1.50

AUDIO CASSETTES
Who the Enemy Is..$4.00
The Occult..$4.00
Rejection...$4.00
Home, Property & Business Cleansing.............$4.00
Deliverance Service..$4.00
Freedom From Bondage (Cassette 4-pack).........$16.00
plus postage and handling................................$1.00

VIDEOCASSETTES
How "They" Got in Me.................................$25.00
Exposing the Occult.....................................$25.00
Rejection..$25.00
plus postage and handling.............................$2.00

To order, call (813) 858-7166, or write us at the following address:

Spiritual Warfare Ministries
P.O. Box 90909
Lakeland, FL 33804-0909

Ken and Nancy Curtis are the founders of Spiritual Warfare Ministries based in Lakeland, Florida. People with behavior, financial, health, emotional, spiritual, or addictive problems are restored each week through their ministry.

The annual Spiritual Warfare Training Conference trains pastors and counselors in all aspects of deliverance and spiritual warfare.